Strengths-Based Changemakers in Education

Strengths-Based Changemakers in Education is the perfect tool for educators looking for brief articles involving the history and current state of racial equity in education. Following each reading, educators can complete self-reflection questions, identify changes needed in their own school, and create a plan of action. The format allows for independent use or with professional learning communities, equity teams, or school improvement planning committees working to interrupt racism in their school.

The book explores different aspects of modern education beginning with a brief history, an understanding of laws and policies and their impact on education, and a dive into how schools are structured. Readers will then consider their own role in education, their school community, and the current state in which they work. Finally, the book considers implementation theory, resistance to change, and dismantling the current to create the new.

For use on its own or in conjunction with the authors' book *Interrupting Racism*, this book lends itself well to use as a guiding resource for equity teams in schools.

Rebecca Atkins is a lifelong educator, nationally board-certified school counselor, and frequent speaker and presenter. She currently serves as a central office administrator in North Carolina.

Alicia K. Oglesby is a high school counselor with over a decade of experience in urban education. She recently began her doctoral studies at The University of Pittsburgh.

"In the face of difficulty and adversity, this book will help the reader to see that opportunities are being brilliantly disguised as impossibilities. Facing the critical need to stand and deliver to those who are actually doing the work and those impeding their progress, this book delivers the mail to the right address."

Dr. Stephen Peters, *President/CEO of The Peters Group and Consultant with Initiative One Leadership Institute*

"*Strengths-Based Changemakers in Education: A Framework for Initiating Systemic Change* is an essential guide for educators committed to racial equity. This book equips individuals and teams with historical insights, self-reflection prompts, and actionable steps to drive meaningful change in their schools. It is a must-read for those ready to take action."

Sheldon L. Eakins, *PhD, author and CEO of the Leading Equity Center*

Strengths-Based Changemakers in Education

A Framework for Initiating Systemic Change

Rebecca Atkins and Alicia K. Oglesby

Routledge
Taylor & Francis Group

NEW YORK AND LONDON

Designed cover image: Getty Images

First published 2026
by Routledge
605 Third Avenue, New York, NY 10158

and by Routledge
4 Park Square, Milton Park, Abingdon, Oxon, OX14 4RN

Routledge is an imprint of the Taylor & Francis Group, an informa business

ISBN: 9781032729374 (hbk)
ISBN: 9781032717418 (pbk)
ISBN: 9781003423126 (ebk)

DOI: 10.4324/9781003423126

Typeset in Adobe Caslon Pro
by KnowledgeWorks Global Ltd.

CONTENTS

INTRODUCTION

Alicia and I met on Twitter, back when it was still known as that. We were both participating in a school counselor chat and got to talking about presenting at our National Conference. We began to DM and decided that we wanted to copresent. This was the 2016 conference in New Orleans and we met for the first time the day before our presentation. While we were there, we were approached by our eventual publisher about writing a book on the topic of our presentation. Two years later, *Interrupting Racism: Equity and Social Justice in School Counseling* (2018) was published.

Since then, we have done countless presentations, keynotes, and talks. We've written articles and have collaborated on this book. We've maintained a professional connection and a friendship. We may go months without talking, but when we do, it's always right where we left off. We wanted to bring that type of conversation to you in a way that prioritizes action. I will text Alicia with a conundrum, she helps me think through it, and I walk away with an idea of action steps. This book includes sections called "Doing the Work" because we want it to inspire you to action rather than passive reading.

Looking back on the work that Alicia and I have done together, we have grown so much. Even though we have combined over 40 years of experience in education, neither of us is an expert but we are practitioners who are constantly working to do better for kids. We hope that this book will help you to do the same.

By nature, I think Alicia and I are positive people who are interested in a strengths-based approach. We always want to focus on the solution rather than the problem. Throughout the book, you'll hear stories of things that went well and ask yourself questions about your own strengths you bring to this work.

The book is organized into eight chapters that will help you to learn about different aspects of education as a system, yourself and your school community, a touch of implementation science, and then action for change. We want to guide you through understanding the system itself – one source of systemic racism that we are working against but we can't stop at admiring the problem, we also have to think about how we can do the work.

In each chapter, the bulk of the text will include learning about the topic. We end that section with key ideas of learning and then move into the Doing the Work section. This section has self-work, collaborative work, and professional learning work. Each of these sections has reflection questions for you, your team, or your school then goes into specific action steps you can take to Doing the Work.

What Rebecca and I offer is a unique blend of learning, reflection, and action. Many textbooks for practitioners and graduate students focus on the learning that educators impart to students. More educational textbooks include valuable action steps, which is necessary for the profession to progress. Rebecca and I talk often and intentionally about making our work actionable *and* reflective, which is hard to do when we don't know who the readers are. Given our serendipitous beginnings working together, I think we found a rhythm. As Rebecca described, we've accomplished a lot together and during that time we've learned a lot about each other and the people with whom we work in our respective roles. We bring that to this book. While we don't claim to have all the answers, we've covered several states and talked with countless educators who share what's missing in professional development. They also share what's missing in conversations with educational leaders. All of their wisdom inspired this book.

This book is meant to help you continue your journey as an educator; a gift of a profession that often leaves people depleted and feeling under-appreciated. We don't have a singular remedy for how the world treats us, but we do have some ideas about how we treat each other and ourselves. We want to persevere. You should grab multicolored sticky notes and pencils so that you can underline, write your thoughts, highlight, and mark text that is most helpful for you at this stage. Then, return to this text in a few years to track your growth and keep moving.

Ultimately, we work with the next generation that is going to shape the world the way they see fit. We hope they shape it for justice.

1

How Did We Get Here?

A Brief History of the State of Race in Education

In this chapter, we will identify the historical events that shape our present-day reality in schools particularly as they pertain to race, school culture, and systemic change over time. Starting with a racialized history is to situate educators within a context relevant to future progress and change we intend to continue and create. The common belief attributed to wise scholars of the past and present reminds us that we must know where we've been to know where we are going. Additionally, we center race and other marginalized identities throughout this book because, as educators and leaders, we know the impact of society on schools and education is ever-present. Because many Americans struggle to discuss race and racism in particular, despite its influence on our everyday lives, we hope to offer our readers more practice at doing difficult tasks. When we can more confidently embrace and dialogue about race, culture, identity, and history, those communication and comprehension skills will make discussions and actions about all areas of our society more approachable.

"The past won't let us go" (Cooper, 2016). The history of education in America is detailed, well-recorded, and specific to race and class. Throughout this book, we plan to examine some of how our educational practices exist because of and about systemic dynamics within America. In this chapter, through the lens of race in particular, we can identify how education functions in the lives of students generally as well as within specific populations, regions, and demographics. Following this chapter are more generalized examples of relevance to your school community. In our first book, we examined changemakers such as education activist Ruby Bridges and the Little Rock Nine, who desegregated their schools despite vicious and dangerous crowds of opposition. Desegregation was a response to over a century of privatized and exclusive education not meant for all children and certainly not meant for or designed for Black and brown children. The history of education in America dates back to what the colonizing class deemed appropriate for a newly formed society. The origins of American education were a means to support the labor force and send specific groups of people to college and leadership roles (Spring, 2018). Education was as much a religious endeavor as a controversial topic. "The minimal instruction in reading and writing given to apprentices was solely for the purpose of teaching religious conformity and conveying an understanding of the laws of the colony" (Spring, 2018, p. 20). Public education for every child was not a part of the plan as this nation was being formed. Therefore, we are invited throughout this book to continue to connect to the more inclusive ideas about why education for all students is necessary and a vital part of our growing society. This is an argument that is still being shaped. We are also invited to remember what we bring to these changing systems, as educational institutions in America are a relatively new concept ripe for improved change.

Throughout this chapter, we will grapple with our understanding of American history, which cannot and must not be separated from race. Be challenged to embrace the continuity of struggles and scholarship related to the American experience of race and education via systems intertwined with numerous aspects of societal life such as housing, immigration, health care, and class. No one event or incident brought us to our present-day moment, but rather, many interrelated and overlapping events that bring us to reading and engaging with this book. A series of unfolding and constantly oscillating human interactions and systemic developments interacted, creating a complex past that we are a part of as well as a product of. This means none of us are separated from history, and none of us are uninfluenced by history. Simply put, we need to know what happened to understand and tackle what is before us in our everyday lives and classrooms.

No one event leads to systemic change within schools. While *Brown v. Board* is a monumental case that sought to provide equal resources and equal opportunities in schools, the legal case was predicated on decades of other legal battles, education advocacy and research, and grassroots efforts stemming from the Civil Rights Movement, abolitionist movements, and labor movements that predated desegregation. This may seem obvious to some, but it is important to note that since this nation's founding, efforts were made to discover an equality that had never been realized in its truest form. As educators, we must witness how change typically happens in American society to learn from it and glean strategies and knowledge from what history teaches us. We can learn about how institutions such as schools take shape and are governed so that we can create or recreate the types of environments where all children can benefit. Experts in education and education history have already paved the way for us to become better acquainted with what has worked in the past to shape a healthier future. Recognition of the issue is one of the first steps in addressing any issue. As we focus on systemic change throughout this book, Dr. Tatum's (1997) words offer practical guidance: When we don't acknowledge systems of advantage, we allow some groups to reap benefits at the cost of other students. The past can act as a guide and a blueprint for the next generations if we allow it.

Some education and teacher programs rightfully draw from the extensive work and research done by experts such as Gloria Ladson-Billings, bell hooks, Lisa Delpit, Shaun Harper, Pedro Noguera, Paulo Freire, Beverly Tatum, and Zoretta Hammond to name a few. These experts will be included throughout this book, and we encourage our readers to study these scholars extensively. These educators and education researchers are contemporary legends in the long legacy of people who study education, systems, and justice. These experts know there is a historical intertwining of race, class, and education that can not and should not be ignored lest we minimize and underestimate the impact of education on students in this country entirely.

While this book does not expect you to become an expert on the intersection of race, culture, and education, we hope everyone reading this book will fully appreciate the moment we find ourselves in today. Please begin or continue to read these authors to further your knowledge.

Let's draw connections between the origins of race in education and our present state of affairs. For the next several examples, we will identify contemporary national issues and show how these issues unfold over time.

Reading Was Illegal for Some

We start at the founding of this nation sometime around the year 1619. The reality of the past 350 years is fairly linear in that the country grew larger by land and population density in a straightforward manner through numerous broken treaties with Indigenous Native Americans. The United States of America was founded on land that is currently and had previously been cultivated by various indigenous communities and tribes. European, mostly Spanish, British, Dutch, Portuguese, and French settlers arrived in North America to create a society that was fueled primarily by the acquisition of land and the exploitation of slave labor (Nkrumah, 1965). This is an incredibly simplistic narration of American history for the sake of brevity, and a fuller, more compelling story of American history can be found in the resource section below if you choose to gain a more comprehensive account. The book *Redesigning Schools to be Antiracist* (Sharp, 2025) clearly details American history as it relates to educational systems. Ultimately, and for the purposes of this chapter, we understand the breaking of treaties between the United States government and indigenous tribes allowed America as a nation to accumulate massive wealth at the expense of enslaved Black people and through the genocide of Indigenous people (Madley, 2016).

Sit with this for a moment. How much of this limited telling of American history did you already know?

What does this history mean to you thus far?

From whose perspective were you taught American history?

Though our account is brief and simplistic, what else might you want to learn about your family's history or your student's history?

History Within and Beyond Our Borders

During the earliest days of this nation, white people in poorer classes toiled in fields earning low wages or debt relief from white plantation owners, but unlike Black and Indigenous people, white indentured

servants were given a pathway to freedom, land ownership, and education. This quickly solidified the chasm between white people and
people of color. So, what does this have to do with us and schools?
Education is a constant across cultures around the globe, replicating
identical structures in labor expectations, what our society expects you
to do with your life, and how we interact with and treat each other. In
other words, education, whether in schools or in the natural environment, is how all people learn. All people across the world learned prior to
the formation of what we now call the United States of America. People
learned differently across the globe based on the needs of their community. This may have looked different in 1492 Japan or 1201 Ghana.
Human societies worldwide have always been educated, and we can learn
many lessons from exploring the history of education beyond our current understanding. Throughout history, education in many facets has
occurred for the benefit of a community of people and their land. For
example, many indigenous tribes throughout North America educated
children to be self-aware and to honor the earth and water as a source
of life for their people (Lomawaima, 1999). While there were and are
many distinctions between various indigenous tribes (i.e., the Lakota
people have different traditions and customs from the Sioux people),
several of our contemporary practices are based on their precolonial
practices. Current state systems, such as the Pennsylvania Department
of Education have entire programming originating from common
Indigenous American practices. The hierarchy of needs we use to
describe care and self-actualization, sometimes as policy, is derived from
the Blackfoot Indian Nation (Feigenbaum & Smith, 2020). Presently,
educators often reference the chart below to tend to student's needs,
not knowing that Maslow studied the practices of Blackfoot Indian
people and those practices influence how we conceptualize student
wellness today.

Oral traditions that span continents such as Africa and Asia can
be found in our practices of circle-time storytelling in kindergarten
classes or elderly guest lecturers in high school courses recounting
their experiences with poll taxes or battles in wars. There are countless
ways in which our present-day occurrences of a school day derive from
centuries-old practices that have proven to contribute to the wellness

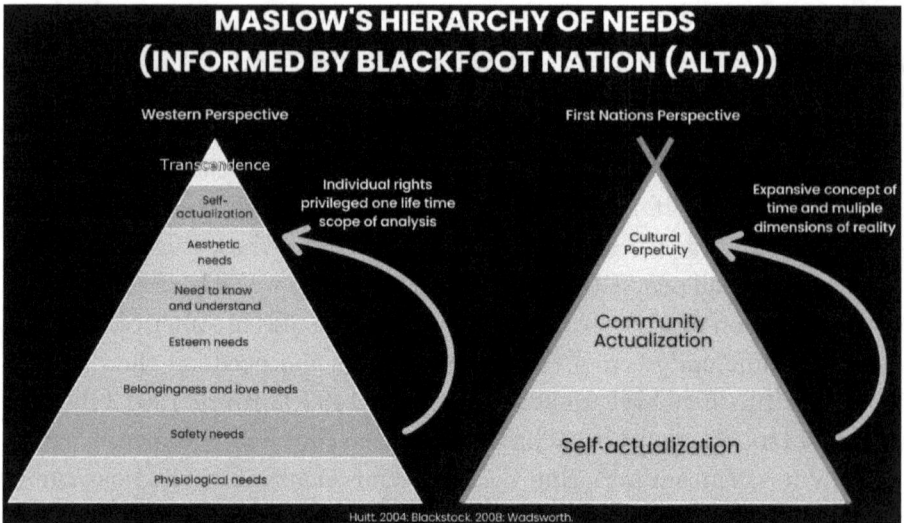

MASLOW'S HIERARCHY OF NEEDS (INFORMED BY BLACKFOOT NATION (ALTA))

Western Perspective

Transcendence
Self-actualization
Aesthetic needs
Need to know and understand
Esteem needs
Belongingness and love needs
Safety needs
Physiological needs

Individual rights privileged one life time scope of analysis

First Nations Perspective

Cultural Perpetuity
Community Actualization
Self-actualization

Expansive concept of time and muliple dimensions of reality

Huitt. 2004: Blackstock. 2008: Wadsworth.

Figure 1.1 (Huitt, 2004). Maslow's hierarchy of needs

and engagement of students (see Figure 1.1). Music in schools and field trips to nature preserves are practices that did not appear from thin air. They are derived from what educators have inherited, either formally or informally, to develop programs that inspire students to want to learn more.

Formalized schooling, as we recognize it contemporarily in American society, began as a European tradition in American colonies. This is to say, settlers came to America and continued schooling practices from their respective European countries, most of which were monarchies at the time. Remember, this is one type of education out of thousands of nations and cultures. The wealthy were expected to learn subjects that would allow them to attend college and lead within their professions. *The Crown* on Netflix, though loosely based on true events in the life of the late Queen Elizabeth, exemplifies this tradition of attending school for a specific purpose: rule or enter the labor force. Given her societal status, she was sent to school to rule as a woman and learn the lessons that would assist her in this role. Historically, laborers "were taught to read and write" at minimum as they pursued their trade or vocation, usually within an apprenticeship model. Does this sound familiar in contemporary society? Are there schools designed to send their students to college, such as college preparatory schools? Are there schools that incorporate career and technical training? These pathways date back to before the origins of this nation. Brought to the newly forming United States of America, the process of education took on traditional European forms as well as new American forms, and yes, some of these new American forms were heavily influenced by democracies of Native American tribes (Lomawaima & McCarty, 2006) because, at the origins of this nation, colonizing settlers had only existed in a monarchy-state. Democracy, including education for all, had to be learned.

In the 1600s and later, Black people were harshly penalized, separated from their families, and even killed for learning to read and write. Learning and teaching to read and write as an enslaved Black person in America was illegal, and anti-literacy laws blanketed most southern states until after the Civil War. Schooling, as a general European and now American tradition, was reserved for certain groups of white children through the eighth grade. Many white laborers didn't see the purpose of being educated as they prioritized work at an early age. Black laborers and enslaved Black people were more demanding about the right to read and be educated. The constant demands led to concepts of education for all (Du Bois, 1935). Schooling happened in a space or building separate from the family, which was traditional for many European colonists but was not customary as a tradition for West African tribes, who had been forced to abandon their cultural practices of learning after being brought to the colonies for enslavement. American public education was eventually funded by the community in which the school existed, and this was a concept that drew favor and contempt. Many white colonial communities were fully invested in financially supporting the learning of all children solely within their community through taxation. A tradition of self-contained education brewed where schools were to benefit the children of that community and only that community. The argument began to spread across the nation that white children in every social class deserved an education, not just the children of wealthy white landowners and college graduates. Therefore, the institution of a free public education as we know it today is still a relatively new concept.

THE ROLE IN EDUCATIONAL HISTORY OF EQUALITY OF OPPORTUNITY AND HUMAN CAPITAL

With the founding of common schools in the early nineteenth century, education was hailed as a means of ending poverty, providing equality of opportunity, and increasing national wealth. These grandiose claims continued into the twentieth century with a strong emphasis on schools selecting students and preparing them for different segments of the labor market. Standardized tests, ability grouping in elementary school classrooms, and the separation of high school students into differing educational programs ranging from college preparatory to vocational training were considered key components in linking schools to the economy.

Joel Spring (2018).

Immigration

Immigration trends begin to shift the characteristics of a new American nation. To this point in history, Black people were forcibly brought to the United States for enslaved labor. They did not willingly travel to the colonies as is customary with immigration. Voluntary immigration can often be connected to a tumultuous home country life and the desire for a safer, calmer, and more financially beneficial future (Massey, 1999). Toward the end of the 1880s, immigration is viewed through the relocation behaviors of Asian people (Ng, 2001). Japanese and Chinese immigrants arrive on American shores, and laws are passed to limit their access, particularly in education, just as anti-literacy laws had been created and passed by state legislators to prevent Black people from learning. All the while, white abolitionists and people of color (Black, Chinese, Japanese, Native Americans, and Latine people) fought adamantly and successfully against these laws. Once the bombing of Pearl Harbor occurred in 1941, schooling for Japanese children drastically changed. Japanese cultural practices were penalized, and classrooms took on the attributes of a nation at war. This change mirrored the "Indian Schools" for Native Indigenous American children who were, and still are, harshly penalized or killed for practicing their cultural traditions. In the spring of 2024, a New Mexico high school refused to allow a Lakota graduate to adorn his graduation attire with feathers and beads, a cultural tradition spanning centuries. Through school policy and practice, these harmful experiences endure in our schools.

The impact of world events, cultural identity, economic pursuits, and numerous other factors serves as a complex web of connections throughout history. Some of the effects can still be seen in our schools today, especially as it pertains to school racial segregation, types of courses and lessons, and the demographics of educators. Much of how and what we learn today is linked to a singular idea of what should happen in school and which students can bring their rich cultural traditions into the learning experience. Can you identify other examples in your community?

Change Happens

Many of the professions dating back to the origins of this nation are the same today, particularly the teacher role. Historically, administrative roles were added as needs shifted and schools' size increased due to the growing population. Once public education became a right within the United States and students were forced to attend school or face truancy consequences (i.e., a compulsory education system), the professional attributes evolved per the needs. For example, formerly known as guidance counselors, school counselors aided in postsecondary planning throughout history. The role solidified in more recent decades to include formal responsibilities that sometimes rely on race and other identity information, such as gender or disability, to create comprehensive school counseling plans. "Guidance" counselors of the past ensured that high school students were prepared for a job. School counselors of the present identify factors within the school that keep groups of students in the margins or at a disadvantage, then work and collaborate to increase access so that all students can achieve the lifestyle they aspire to have. Over time, the roles evolved to meet the needs of an evolving society. The same is true for classroom teachers. The evolution of teacher curriculum was also met with the philosophy of equity, where various types of instruction took place in many different types of schools. Project-based learning, traditional lecture-style classes, standardized lessons, and Montessori-style instruction, to name a few, all spoke to the shift in meeting students' needs rather than students conforming to one way of schooling. Over time, the justification for social-emotional learning and critical thinking skills became more apparent. Children no longer left middle or high school to work alongside their parents and guardians in factories, and schools' evolving nature demonstrated that change.

Free Education

In 1818, one of the first publicly funded and controlled education districts originated in Philadelphia to create resources for the city's children to be educated and accounted for. As you may have guessed, schools were mostly racially segregated and segregated by gender during this time (Cutler, 2012). There were schools in Philadelphia like the Institute for Colored Youth for Black children and schools like Central High School for white male teenagers where education was free. Students were also no longer dependent on their neighborhood or neighbors to provide a free education. Allocated financial resources throughout American history have meant that adults can be hired to educate children and support the school building's efforts and initiatives. Where communities suffered from brutal poverty, education also suffered. Providing free and appropriate education to any child from any area of the city or town was a monumental endeavor for this new nation.

Additionally, the contemporary burdens of high teacher turnover and politicizing of teachers' roles are not a new occurrence. This is an important note to remember because as this nation seeks to define and reflect a democratic society more accurately, educators have been and continue to be deliberate in the call for the right to a free and appropriate public education since the founding of this nation. As different cultures and ethnicities share their values and traditions within and beyond our borders, educators are privy to the vast ways of communicating and teaching beyond and in addition to the ways of white European settlers. More formally known as ethnic studies, a contemporary term for learning through the lens of different cultures, educators and administrators have ongoing advocacy aims. First, they must decide how to teach the students in their building, which is, again, not a new phenomenon. This will be an ever-changing characteristic of education, where educators learn from the past to inform better practices for the future. That journey will forever be present, especially as cultures of the world move into and around the United States. Second, educators must also advocate for public education for all children. In many cultures worldwide, such as precolonial Nigeria, communities used what we might think of as an equivalent to Montessori-style learning for all children starting at 5 years old. China also educated almost all of its citizens during dynasties dating back to 1600 B.C. So, while educating all children in society is nothing new globally, it is more recent for the United States, a newer nation, and thus ripe for strengthening via the lessons of the past and present.

Sociopolitical Context

Another constant in our world of education, as teachers and leaders, is context. We've thus far reviewed a quick, multicultural historical account of the American context. Education in America was and is shaped by the political context as well, such as who is the president or the mayor. The social context, such as cell phone addiction or the popularity of athletics, also impacts us today as it has shaped us through our history. Other factors certainly impact how and what is taught, but let's momentarily focus on these two factors in combination. Sociopolitical expert Eddie Glaude Jr. shares that we can't afford to be unaware and uninformed about what impacts our students and school communities. Some may challenge the notion of sociopolitical awareness in education by stating, "Why does education have to be political?" The answer is simply that education is created by policy, and policy is impacted by politics. American states such as North Carolina, Georgia, Virginia, Alabama, and Louisiana literally enforced laws where only Black people were not allowed to read and write. History is incredibly detailed if we are willing to face harsh truths. A nation doesn't function without rules, and education is no different than any other organized institution in our society where laws dictate what happens in school buildings. Schools can not be exempt from governance. Educational laws will be further explained in later chapters, so in preparation for continued reading, think of your school and its sociopolitical context:

1. Has immigration impacted your neighborhood? How so?
2. Is your school racially integrated? If so, why? If not, why not?

3. Are the parents in your school community more Democrats, Republicans, or somewhere in the middle? Has this been true throughout your school's history?

4. Are your ancestors from your current hometown? How many generations can you connect to your current location? Who migrated to the United States and why?

Numerous factors contribute to our school's history and how our schools have been shaped over time, including laws, identity expression, technology, and even climate changes that require some communities, such as New Orleans, to reinvent their entire school system. The goal of this section is to illustrate how connected we are to the past and our context. When we are honest about that impact and that history, we see there are battles and successes we have made in education that we can continue to fight and succeed if we have the right tools.

Melody Kramer (2024) documents a time after the 1954 *Brown v. Board* ruling in her community's history that led to schools being built and maintained over decades (Figure 1.2). She accounts for the history of these schools in a 2024 blog story. It reads:

The Pearsall Plan to Save our Schools, as it was called, was a way to allow students to be excused from attending integrated public schools. In other words, to stall desegregation in North Carolina. It passed with 80% support. Kramer continues by explaining how over half of Chapel Hill didn't approve of this plan which was in part due to Black residents. The plan passed and two elementary schools became the focus. One of the schools would be designed for Black children and another for white children. Brown v Board had already passed. Racial segregation in schools was deemed unconstitutional, yet Chapel Hill was actively planning and developing two racially segregated schools. Kramer notes that organizations such as The Chapel Hill Fellowship for School Integration fought against the Pearsall Plan, wanting to align with the country's movement toward racial justice for all

Figure 1.2 Chapel Hill Weekly: Move Aims to Block Construction.

children. Led by Black clergymen, the fight for integration was pursued by fewer Chapel Hill residents than those against integration. This is a testament to how unpopular racial justice has been throughout this country's history despite relentless efforts to make liberty and justice a reality for all. Creating a societal system, let alone a school system, where equitable interventions are central to policies and daily procedures means embarking on practices that have yet to be fully realized. Fortunately, we can learn from the past.

As demonstrated in Kramer's historical account, shaping and shifting systems is an ongoing project school leaders and community members have engaged in, particularly race-related. The connection to a history of anti-literacy laws is no coincidence but a continuation of policies, practices, and beliefs. America is not a colorblind society, and we must confront the details of our educational systems if we should hope to influence them in healthier ways for all students. As evidenced by Kramer's North Carolina area and the sweeping educational shifts in New Orleans, moving from a centrally directed public school district to the first majority charter school city in the country, the factors contributing to systemic change are vast but known. Erasing this history deprives us of imagining an education system where all students feel liberated. Change is inevitable, but as educators, we must ensure the change we embrace has the most positive effects on children as possible. Being honest and knowledgeable about how systems evolve is a first step.

Default Racism

History has given us institutions made up of customs, practices, traditions, and people that may or may not be serving the best interests of the students or professionals within that school. As this chapter concludes, we again invite you to deepen your knowledge about the history of education through various texts. Our summation doesn't do justice to the incredible insights and connections available in our resource and references sections.

Finally, we must attend to the embedded racism within education not only through racial segregation but also through the often unintentional policies and practices inherent in our schools.

> What happens when we don't activate a community of care and justice while recognizing the automated and automatic default to racism?
>
> (author unknown)

As stated throughout this chapter, we see how race influences the origins of our present-day disparities within the field of education. From enslaved Black people being punished or killed for reading and writing to the constant antagonization of affirmative action, which are steps to counter historical and current discriminatory practices intentionally, education is a hotbed for racist practices that often go unnoticed. Throughout this book, we will tackle this issue and other issues of identity in schools.

Race and racism are embedded within the fabric of our society, and not only must we acknowledge and respect that truth, but we must also actively undo its harm on ourselves and our students. Default racism means that a system or structure is created using features that explicitly discriminate against groups of people based on their skin color. A commonly known example of this is redlining, which is now deemed illegal in housing practices (Massey & Denton, 1993). Redlining was once a legal practice to limit homeownership in specific wealthier white communities. Signs at the entrance of cul de sacs greeted visitors explicitly stating that the neighborhood was "For Whites Only." Black, Latine, Asian, and Jewish families, despite their ability to pay or military veteran status, were denied access to these communities and homes for generations. Homeownership and community demographics defaulted to racism. This, in turn, affected schools because neighborhood schools reflected the neighborhood. When the reality of socioeconomic class enters the conversation, educators must be knowledgeable about the overlap of race and class. Whether through teacher preparation programs or other certification measures, these historical facts must be confronted as they relate to schools. Socioeconomic class in America is directly linked to race and racism. Redlining is a primary example of how the two characteristics are inextricably linked. Numerous examples are scattered throughout decades of research. Gaps in educational opportunities, health outcomes, and employment rates consistently mark race, a social construct and by no means an actual biological fact, as a determining factor, even when class is constant. While class and race often contribute to the well-being of students and educators, we do not need to separate the two. Both impact lives. Educators often see this in discipline outcomes and advanced course enrollment. In essence, because races of people have more in common biologically than uncommon, we know that people are treated differently because of how they are perceived and how we create meaning about how those perceptions should affect people's lives. In systems that are unequal across race and class lines, and where student populations are continuing to grow more divers, educators must precisely address which acts help equalize opportunity for various students of color, because educators are often inundated with vague practices about how to treat students of color "equally" in schools: "celebrate diversity!" "pursue equity!" "don't be colorblind!" (Pollock, 2008). Perceptions about race impact the creation of schools, classrooms, lessons, and ultimately entire systems. If people can create the parameters to maintain a racist society, we can create the parameters to dismantle a racist society. "Educators need to keep asking a basic question: which of our everyday acts move specific students or student populations toward educational opportunity, and which acts move them farther away from it?" (Pollock, 2008)

Glean from the Experts

Throughout her research, Dr. Gloria Ladson-Billings describes the educational debt owed to children of America. She draws on examples of the past, such as enslavement of Black families, mission schools separating Native American children from their families and cultures, and Latinx students being denied the right to "an equitable and high-quality education." A key point from her research challenges educators to imagine our future as a nation if we continue to deny all students access to empowering learning.

Take a moment to envision two scenarios:

1. A society where every student has easy and convenient access to all they want and need to learn and achieve their self-identified goals.
2. A society where students and their families have to spend countless hours fighting for basic educational needs.

Share your thoughts through journaling or with a colleague.

What do you see when you envision the first case:

What do you see when you envision the second case:

bell hooks (2014) shows us foundational ways we must engage as educators. With love, compassion, and intention at the center, hooks reminds teachers, administrators, and leaders of all kinds that children are the soul of every community, particularly schools. She tells us that we must be interested in one another and willing to listen to one another if we hope to achieve any semblance of a unified educational environment. This includes an acknowledgment of our different and shared histories.

In the coming chapters, we'll address educational law, critical race theory, increasing positive school culture through anti-racist practices, and so much more. Get your notebooks, journals, and educator teams together to walk through this text as you learn and grow and hopefully become empowered to create the change we need to see.

As we continue to learn from the past, may we be inspired by all that we imagine can be better tomorrow.

Key Ideas:

- American history is relevant in understanding our current state of education.
- Lessons from the past will help us understand why we are in our present circumstances and how we can imagine better systems from previous societies.
- Race and racism greatly and deeply impact how American society functions despite calls and legislation to erase historical context.
- By becoming more familiar with conversations about race and racism, we are more prepared to handle the urgency of creating better schools.

Doing the Work

In each Doing the Work section, we will take the learning from the chapter and apply it to self-work, collaborative work, and professional learning work. To impact change, we must do the work.

Self-Work:

1. What is the history of education in your family? Be sure to ask your elders for their insights and memories.
2. Was your school desegregated? If so, was it evident in the makeup of your classes? Detail these memories.
3. Find an elder in your community or in your circle of a different race from you and ask permission to interview them about their experiences in school as they pertain to race: Was your school desegregated? What were the families' responses to the school community? Were classes integrated or racially diverse? What

was your community's response to that? Do you believe much has changed? Why or why not?

4. Commit to a learning team or community. Review this text and other texts together. Ask each other questions and hold each other accountable for learning growth.

Journal to Yourself:

1. Do you believe that Black and brown children should have clean, safe, and well-constructed schools? Or should they do something specific to earn this?

2. In our first book, we briefly described the bell curve and how educators assume underachievement of students was often related to race and not class or treatment of students by adults. Do you believe in the bell curve and that in order for some students to achieve, some students must fail? What does the data at your school tell you about commonalities between groups of students who perform poorly? What stories do you create related to this data?

3. What role does race and/or class play at your school? If none, your institution is either an anomaly and must be studied for research or feelings, perceptions, and attitudes about race may be kept hidden within certain groups. How can you uncover the truth?

Collaborative Work

Collaborate with your local high school's history department on topics related to race and culture within your local community; research your own school's history and how you are situated within that history, your family, your grandparents, and their grandparents – give an example of someone who may have integrated a school in your town or the nearest town.

Tour your local museum with colleagues and ask questions related to the self-work questions above. Share your learning journey with the museum curator or tour guide.

Read: *The Warmth of Other Suns* by Isabel Wilkerson
Read: *A People's History of the United States: 1492-Present* by Howard Zinn

Read: *A Forgotten Sisterhood: Pioneering Black Women Educators and Activists in the Jim Crow South* by Audrey Thomas McCluskey

Discuss these books as a book study group and how they relate to this chapter.

At your local library, find three books and one map of your school's community 50 years ago or more.

Professional Learning Work

Find a local education historian webinar and share it during a faculty and staff meeting to view and discuss or bring in a local historian for a portion of your next professional development day to share the history of your school and the neighborhood that surrounds it.

Invite a local politician to your school to discuss the contents of this chapter and your self-work journey. Ask questions about the laws in your community and how they impact your school. Build a collaborative rapport for future advocacy efforts to be discussed in later chapters.

A special "thank you" to Black Girl Magic at the University of Pittsburgh, School of Education, for compiling notes contributed to this chapter's thinking.

Additional Resources and Readings

bell hooks' *Teaching to Transgress* is required reading.

Paulo Freire's *Pedagogy of the Oppressed* is required reading.

Zinn, H. (2015). *A people's history of the United States: 1492–present.* Routledge.

Seeing White. Scene on Radio Podcast: https://sceneonradio.org/seeing-white/

Sharp, S. (2025). *Redesigning schools to be antiracist: A systemic change approach for school counselors and other leaders.* Corwin Press.

Gloria Ladson-Billings. From the Achievement Gap to the Education Debt: Understanding Achievement in U.S. Schools Author(s): Gloria Ladson-Billings Source: Educational Researcher, Vol. 35, No. 7 (2006, October), pp. 3–12 Published by: American Educational Research Association Stable URL: https://www.jstor.org/stable/3876731 Accessed: October 22, 2018 21:40 UTC.

References

Cooper, B. (2016). *The racial politics of time*. TED Women Video.

Cutler, W. III (2012). *Public education: The school district of Philadelphia—The encyclopedia of greater Philadelphia*. Rutgers.

Du Bois, W. B. (1935). Does the negro need separate schools? *Journal of Negro Education*, *4*(3), 328–335.

Feigenbaum, K. D., & Smith, R. A. (2020). Historical narratives: Abraham Maslow and Blackfoot interpretations. *The Humanistic Psychologist*, *48*(3), 232.

hooks, b (2014). *Teaching to transgress*. Routledge.

Kramer, M. (2024). *Blog entry*. https://triangleblogblog.com/2024/07/21/when-chapel-hill-fought-school-desegregation-the-racist-origins-of-frank-porter-graham-elementary-school/?fbclid=IwY2xjawEOB8tleHRuA2FlbQIxMQABH eGYSbjElvUh7k-Z5p4Sitv0SP3LNPjpT1ShUN3B3QjfD3PF3NMESvk6nA_aem_4Hpdkqlasp5fcqLxn7r6LQ

Lomawaima, K. T. (1999). *The unnatural history of American Indian education*. Blackwell Publishing.

Lomawaima, K. T., & McCarty, T. L. (2006). *"To remain an Indian": Lessons in democracy from a century of native American education*. Teachers College Press.

Madley, B. (2016). *An American genocide: The United States and the California Indian catastrophe, 1846-1873*. Yale University Press.

Massey, D. S. (1999). *Why does immigration occur?: A theoretical synthesis* (pp. 34–52). The Handbook of International Migration.

Massey, D. S., & Denton, N. A. (1993). *American apartheid*. Harvard.

Ng, W. (2001). *Japanese American internment during World War II: A history and reference guide*. Bloomsbury Publishing.

Nkrumah, K. (1965). *Neo-colonialism*. Nelson.

Pollock, M. (Ed.). (2008). *Everyday antiracism: Getting real about race in school*. The New Press.

Sharp, S. (2025). *Redesigning schools to be antiracist: A systemic change approach for school counselors and other leaders*. Corwin Press.

Spring, J. (2018). *The American school: From the Puritans to the Trump era*. Taylor & Francis Group.

Tatum, B. D. (1997). *Why are all the black kids sitting together in the cafeteria?* Basic Books.

2

EDUCATION IN YOUR STATE AND COMMUNITY

When working in a school building, you have a number of influential groups: parents, staff, administrators, students, and even community members. As educators, we often spend our time talking about these groups and considering their values, opinions, norms, and needs. However, decision-making at the school, committee, or individual level happens within the context of law and policy. We cannot talk about how we will impact change within our building until we consider the important aspect of educational decision-making in federal, state, and local government.

> It is the civil society leaders who, in many ways, are going to have the more lasting impact," President Obama said. "Because as the saying goes, the most important title is not 'president' or 'prime minister'; the most important title is 'citizen.'

> (Somander, 2014)

Federal Education Impact

Before the Elementary and Secondary Education Act (ESEA) of 1965, the federal government had minimal involvement in K-12 education. The move to increase involvement began with a court decision:

DOI: 10.4324/9781003423126-2

the 1954 *Brown v. Board of Education* that has been interpreted to give the federal government the power to intervene in cases of legally sanctioned discrimination, like the segregation of public schools across the country; to mandate equal access to education for students with disabilities; and, according to some arguments, to correct for persistently unequal access to resources across states and districts of different income levels.

(Pelsue, 2017)

The ESEA offered funding to states based on certain conditions as designated by sections, or titles, of the act. The titles will be familiar to you: Title I offered funds for schools with a large percentage of low-income students, Title VI for children with disabilities, and Title VII for bilingual education. This allowed the federal government to influence K-12 education without overriding states' rights.

Over the years, the government has continued to add funding and conditions to the ESEA Act but no more than the 2001 No Child Left Behind Act (NCLB). The NCLB Act emphasized standardized testing, adequate yearly progress, and rigorous standards. Many criticized the law for overemphasizing "teaching to the test," unrealistic expectations, and ignoring the disparities evident in standardized testing. ESEA was reauthorized in 2015 with the Every Student Succeeds Act (ESSA), leaving intact the use of standardized testing but moving the evaluation and accountability mandates to the states.

In the push-pull of states' rights vs federal mandates, a force outside of the law can work to influence change. This "bully pulpit" can include presidential remarks, executive orders, and Dear Colleague letters. Presidential rhetoric extends influence over public opinion, congressional debate, and agency involvement in hot-button topics. One can look most recently at the presidencies of Obama, Trump, and Biden to see examples of their commentary on education in relation to the current climate.

Presidents use executive orders to influence change. President Obama (2012) and President Biden (2021) signed executive orders with the purpose of Advancing Education Equity, Excellence, and Economic Opportunity for Black Americans (U.S. Department of Education, n.d.).

In 2020, Trump signed an executive order Expanding Educational Opportunity through School Choice (Trump White House Archives, 2020). These executive orders direct federal agencies' work (and funding) and clarify or extend laws. When the executive office changes, the new president can revoke previous orders, making executive orders more easily changed than laws passed by Congress.

The president can direct agencies to issue educational reports to influence Congress and promote their agenda. In 1983, under Ronald Reagan, the White House published the report "Nation at Risk" that promoted the idea that schools were failing and that educational reform was needed. In *Punished for Dreaming,* Dr. Bettina Love outlines how this report ushered in the far right's education agenda and impacted education to this day (Love, 2023).

The "Dear Colleague Letter" is a form of guidance issued by agencies, including the Department of Education and the Office of Civil Rights (OCR), to guide how laws and policies are implemented. When a new administration comes into office, they may direct that "Dear Colleague Letters" be rescinded and new guidance issued. Because of this, it's helpful to stay on top of current guidance.

An example of this is Dear Colleague Letters regarding transgender students in schools. In May 2016, the Obama administration issued a letter stating, "When a school provides sex-segregated activities and facilities, transgender students must be allowed to participate in such activities and access such facilities consistent with their gender identity" (Lhamon & Gupta, 2016). In February 2017, this letter was rescinded under the Trump Administration. As of publication, the 2017 Dear Colleague letter is under review and states "UNDER REVIEW (as of April 30, 2021). This document and the underlying issues are under review in light of Executive Order 13988 on Preventing and Combating Discrimination on the Basis of Gender Identity or Sexual Orientation and recent (court) case law. OCR and CRT are committed to ensuring that all students, including LGBTQ students, are able to learn and thrive in a safe environment. Please note that this notation does not have the effect of reinstating prior guidance" (Battle & Wheeler, 2017).

Federal agencies issue regulations in a process called "rulemaking." This is a long process that includes many phases: initiating rule-making, developing proposed rules, and developing final rules. In early 2024, the Department of Education issued regulations related to Title IX that definitively stated that sexual orientation and gender identity are protected characteristics. This applies to all forms of sexual discrimination at federally funded educational institutions except athletics, which is handled by a separate regulation. The regulation would apply to access to bathrooms and locker rooms, dress codes, dance dates, and many more. Unlike guidance and Dear Colleague Letters, regulations have the force of law. Congress can overturn a federal rule within 60 days through the Congressional Review Act (CRA). Alternatively, a federal court could suspend the law while litigation is happening, but the regulations cannot be changed without another rulemaking process. As of this publication, Congress failed to pass the CRA resolution against Title IX, though it did pass the House. Preliminary injunctions are currently in place in some federal districts.

State Education Law

Media can often focus on federal-level policies and laws, but educators seeking to effect building-level change should consider state laws and local policies to see a more immediate impact. The federal government uses its financial resources to influence K-12 education, but states have the direct authority to determine local education. Each state can vary, but we will consider an overview of how education laws and policies are proposed, debated, and enacted at the state level.

Education laws and policies are initiated by a variety of influences, including educational agencies, advocacy groups, lobbyists, and citizens. The state legislator or group of legislators will sponsor bills that align with their interests. At this point, the bill is introduced in one of the chambers of the state legislature and assigned to the relevant committee, often an education committee. The committee reviews the bill and may make amendments.

The committee may hold public hearings and debate the bill, which leads to changes and amendments. The bill must pass through the committee before going to the full legislative body. Once the bill is presented for debate in the full chamber, further amendments may be proposed. Finally, a vote is taken, and if the majority of members in that chamber approve, it will proceed to the other chamber, going through a similar process of committee, debate, and voting.

If both chambers approve the final bill, it is sent to the governor for approval or veto. Once the bill becomes law, it is the responsibility of the state board of education, school districts, and other educational institutions to implement and comply with the new law. This often takes a long process of considering the implications of laws often written by lawmakers who are not themselves educators, such as class size laws that don't consider the number of physical classrooms available for use. Having a small K-3 classroom sounds great, but if most of our buildings are at capacity, it's not simple to put in place. As an educator, there are many moments of advocacy and influence, including legislators, advocacy groups, committee members, and the governor.

Examples of State Education Policies

As educators working toward systemic change, several areas of state law and policy are key concerns: curriculum standards, assessment requirements, funding formulas, teacher certification and licensure, and school accountability measures. We will talk more about funding formulas in Chapter 3.

A recent push in "parents' rights" bills limits conversations around race, gender, and sexuality. States, such as Texas, Tennessee, and North Dakota, have laws prohibiting Diversity, Equity, and Inclusion topics in professional development for teachers (American Speech Language Hearing Association, n.d.). In 2022, six states prevent race, bias, or identity from being included in curriculum (USA Facts, 2023). According to the Movement Advance Project, 40% of LGBTQ youth live in a state where LGBTQ-related curriculum is limited or not allowed. In each of these instances, teachers are changing what they teach, students' school experiences are changed, and the impact of both is real (Movement Advancement Project, n.d.).

School Board Policies

School boards are local governing bodies that govern the work of the school system. When federal and state law impacts the work of schools, it is the school board's responsibility to determine policies and procedures that ensure that the school system is following the laws.

Somewhere between state or federal law and school board policies is often a state board or department of education that interprets laws. This agency will issue guidance that supports local education agencies (LEAs) in applying the law. Laws are not usually written by educators and sometimes don't immediately make sense in application. This can cause confusion as LEAs don't know how to respond immediately. School boards will sometimes wait to change policies until guidance is issued both from the state agency and from their legal teams.

School boards also create many policies that are not related to a state or federal law. One example that is prevalent in the news today – book bans. Book bans have reached historic levels, and districts across the nation are creating processes and procedures to respond to requests for removal of materials from classrooms and libraries. Some teachers are required to submit a list of every book in their classrooms, and others have to wait for those lists to be approved before allowing students to access books. Not only does this impact student access to literature, it takes time away from the other tasks of school librarians, teachers, counselors, and administrators.

School board meetings often have low attendance, and many community members may not know when important decisions are being made. We would argue that your advocacy can make the most profound impact at the local level. When your school board hears from parents, students, teachers, counselors, and administrators about how their policies impact daily life at school, they are better able to create policies that support all students.

Education Reform and the Impact on Students of Color

It is important to consider impact separate from intention when considering education law and policies. Because of the bias of the humans working within the system, and the racism seeped into how the educational system works, well-intentioned education reform can have a disproportionately negative impact on students of color. It's necessary to call out that at times, reform is not well-intentioned and that the system is working as it was designed. One of my colleagues, Kate Kennedy, has a saying, "it is not an opportunity gap, it's a moat." Let's explore one example of educational reform that disproportionately impacted students of color. This is far from an exhaustive list.

Data indicates that Black students are more likely to be punished more harshly for less serious infractions than their white peers. Black boys are impacted at an even higher rate. Black boys account for 8% of all students, but 19% of the students expelled, often without educational services (Ford, 2021).

A few years ago, some colleagues and I dove deep into discipline referrals as an example of data-based problem-solving in a professional development we were designing. We quickly noticed a pattern where Black boys were written up and disciplined for things where other students would probably receive a light rebuke. One example that stands out in my mind is a boy who had high grades, high scores on the SEL Screener, but a number of discipline referrals. Most of the discipline referrals were things like "fighting in the hallway." We took the time to read the write-ups and saw that the "fights" were with friends and no one was hurt. One even said something like the boys were laughing and smiling when brought to the office. That's also called roughhousing. These were middle school boys; roughhousing is completely developmentally appropriate and could have been redirected with a reminder. Though I don't know for sure, I imagine that many other kids were roughhousing and did not receive discipline referrals. The district where I worked at the time did not have a zero-tolerance policy, but I believe that disparities like this example stem from the prevalence of such policies.

Zero-tolerance discipline policies were designed to "keep students safe" by requiring predetermined consequences for different infractions. The rise of zero tolerance came primarily after Columbine and other mass violence at schools in the 1990s but began in the 1980s as a "response to fears about increasing school violence" (MindShift, 2016). No surprise that this might happen after the Reagan-era *Nation at Risk*. When implementing discipline consequences, there was no room for context. For example, a second grader ate his Pop-Tart and said, "Look it's a gun." He was suspended for two days (St. George, 2016).

Community Engagement

Now that you have considered how federal and state law and board policy impact your day-to-day life at school, consider how you might engage your school community in amplifying the voice of students, families, and educators.

What is community engagement? The CDC defines community engagement as:

> The process of working collaboratively with and through groups of people affiliated by geographic proximity, special interest, or similar situations to address issues affecting the well-being of those people. It is a powerful vehicle for bringing about environmental and behavioral changes that will improve the health of the community and its members. It often involves partnerships and coalitions that help mobilize resources and influence systems, change relationships among partners, and serve as catalysts for changing policies, programs, and practices.
>
> (Clinical and Translational Science
> Awards Consortium, 2011)

The idea of working "with and through" is a powerful one. Be mindful that the Supreme Court ruled that public employees do not have First Amendment protection for speech issued as part of their official duties (*Garcetti v. Ceballos*, 2006). As engaged citizens, we work with our communities to seek change through law and policy. As school employees, we work through community groups (outside of working hours!) to seek change through law and policy. In order to do both, we will need to consider our influence capital.

In this instance, influence capital refers to the assets that we possess that can influence decision-makers to change or maintain laws, policies, and practices. Within this idea, we have the interest–influence grid.

High interest, low influence	High interest, high influence
Low interest, low influence	Low interest, high influence

Low interest, low influence: This group includes people who may not be highly interested in your area of concern and also have little to no influence in changing the policy or practice. Keep this group in the know as they may become more interested or gain influence over the course of your work. However, do not spend too much time and communication effort that takes away from other groups.

High interest, low influence: This group includes people who are highly interested in your concern but have little to no influence in changing it. You might think that you don't need to spend time with this group, but their influence level could be indirect or amplified. Student groups may not be able to vote in elections, but they can speak about and change community mindsets. Their influence can be indirect rather than direct. Likewise, groups of people can have a powerful voice that individuals do not have. Add to either scenario a powerful ally, and you have changemakers.

Low interest, high influence: This group is typically people or groups in power, like your principal, school board member, or lawmakers. It's not that they don't have any interest in your cause, but they have many causes that are seeking their attention. While you will be working to increase their interest level, it's also very important to keep them informed so that they don't use their influence to work against your cause. This can happen when misinformation is spread or they don't have enough information.

High interest, high influence: This is your most engaged group. They are interested in your cause and would likely benefit from it. They also have influence over the decision or change itself. This is the group you want to highly engage. Here is where you spend your energy and time for your cause. We often spend time working hard to change levels of influence and interest without maximizing the work of those who are already engaged.

Key Ideas:

- **Influence of federal education law:** Federal law impacts education through funding. While federal law is slow to change, departmental guidance, presidential orders, and influence at the federal level do impact schools.

- **State education law and policy**: Federal laws influence education, but states play a critical role in determining local education policies, including curriculum standards, assessment requirements, and funding formulas. State law governs school board policy.
- **Impact of school board policies**: School boards, as local governing bodies, interpret and implement federal and state laws, shaping the daily experiences of students and educators. Community engagement with school boards can influence policy decisions that directly impact schools and communities.
- **Community engagement and influence capital:** Engaging with communities can amplify the voices of students, families, and educators in shaping education policy. Understanding influence capital and targeting efforts toward groups with high interest and influence can be key in effecting change at local and state levels.

Doing the Work

In each Doing the Work section, we will take the learning from the chapter and apply it to self-work, collaborative work, and professional learning work. To impact change, we must do the work.

Self-Work

When considering law and policy, self-work is a critical component. Being an educator doesn't allow for time and space to advocate for law and policy change as part of our job. While we might advocate in the evenings or on the weekends, we're not going to be able to, for example, promote a particular candidate's platform in the middle of a Professional Learning Community (PLC).

One of the aspects that we will have to grapple with is what to do if we don't agree with the law. A simple example would be standardized testing. I have yet to meet an educator who thinks that statewide standardized testing is beneficial to students. At the same time, most choose to work around it by promoting whole-child learning and de-emphasizing the importance of one test in their own classroom or building.

A more complex example would be when a law is in place that you believe is punitive or unethical. In my state, we have a parents' rights bill that requires schools to notify parents when their child asks to go by a different name. I believe that this law outs children and may create unsafe environments in their homes. However, I am still required to uphold the law. I have many choices available to me. I could leave the profession, I could break the law (and risk being fired in a state with no union), and I could determine ways to follow the law that protect children the best that I can. In order to make this decision, I will need to reflect deeply through self-work in relation to law and policy.

What are your core values of education? Why did you choose to become an educator?

No matter what our core values are, we have to work within the education system as it exists. The system differs from state to state and community to community.

What laws can you identify that impact your practice?

What policies can you identify that impact your practice?

Are there any laws or policies that counter your ethical standards? How have you pushed up against these laws in your work?

Now that you've considered the surrounding environment of the school system where you work, consider the system itself. Describe your school board. If you are unable to do so, consider attending a meeting or watching a few meetings online.

What kinds of policy is your school board likely to prioritize?

What values does the school board promote, and do their votes align with those values?

In some settings, there are rules and then there are unwritten rules. We'll explore that more in future chapters. But it's worth considering law and policy within the context of the unwritten rules.

What are the political climate factors that impact your school community that may not be captured in law and policy?

What is your role in laws and policies?

What is your role in applying law and policy?

We are not interested in being integrated into this value structure.
~Martin Luther King, Jr.

What are the values you want to change in your school or community? How do law and policy impact that change?

Are there changes within your own actions that need to change to embody the change?

Who are your allies and co-conspirators in this work? They could be within your school building, community, or professional learning network.

Action:
- Attend a school board meeting.
- Write a politician about a law that impacts your students.
- Write your school board about a policy that impacts your students.
- Join local nonprofits that support change in education law.
- Register to attend an "On the Hill" day at your state capitol.

Collaborative Work

If you haven't taken the time to review the board policy section of your district website, use the search function to look up key words that are related to your work day to day. For example, grading, attendance, or counseling. If you have reviewed board policies previously, take the time to carefully read key board policies. Review three board policies and discuss:

How does this connect to state and federal law?

What connections can we make to our school community in relation to these policies?

Are there policies that we would like to see changed? How can we gather our collective voice to seek this change?

What ways do we connect with families to determine what is important to them right now regarding their child's education?

In what ways are we perpetuating negative practices in our work with students and families? Are there times that we don't apply policies equally between groups? Are there times when we follow policy without pausing to ensure there is no harm?

Action:

- Present collective recommendations to your principal or other decision-makers about changes that would positively impact students.
- Change the informal policies within your department or PLC that inequitably impact students.
- Collaborate to collect data to determine how policies are inequitably impacting students.

Professional Learning Work

Take the time to complete a policy audit in your building. This may be formal policies directly from the school board or practices/informal policies within your building.

Choose a Policy

Perhaps you're not sure where to start. Consider a policy or practice that you've heard complaints about from students, seen data that is disproportionate, or even that you just don't think works well.

Ask and Listen

Talk to students, families, fellow colleagues, and leaders about what they notice about the policy or practice. Listen (really listen!) to what they say about their experiences. Gather anecdotal data to share with decision-makers. Discovering how policies harm students requires brave honesty about the impact of rules on the lives of students. Be open and aware that as part of the system, we are also a part of what might be causing harm. Stay willing to confront the idea in order to create change.

Collect Data

Schools function on data. Collect as much quantitative data as possible. Show disproportionality or relate the policy or practice to outcomes. Does the data show that girls are more likely to be dress coded? Does the school's registration process mean that not all students have access to higher level courses? Paint the picture as clearly as possible.

Gather Your Team

Enroll the assistance of other school faculty, staff, administrators, students, and families to strengthen your efforts. Be sure the colleagues participating in the audit understand the source of the problem. Be careful to not "problematize" students or make students the root of issues in your school. For example, low enrollment of multilingual students in the gifted program does not mean those students are not gifted or not interested but rather the tools measuring giftedness are not capturing multilingual giftedness. Your team should recognize the distinction. The system impacting your students is usually the source.

Reflect

Be open to the possibility that your ideas may not work or may inflict a different type of harm. Evaluation is key! Stay in contact with students and families to gauge the impact of change and be ready to make changes from your original plan. Continue to collect and interpret data through a social justice lens.

How is the policy implemented in your building?

Is implementation equal among all groups of students?

Do certain groups of students disproportionately benefit from or suffer from the policy?

Does the policy itself make sense, but the implementation is uneven, without fidelity, or based on opt-in or opt-out language?

If you could wave a magic wand and change the policy or its outcome in some way, what would the new policy or procedure be?

Action:

- Hold your colleagues and administrators accountable for equitable enforcement of policy.
- Advocate for changes related to written policies and procedures.
- Write to your school board or attend a school improvement team meeting; do this in groups if possible to highlight the support for a change.
- Collaborate to collect data to determine how policies are inequitably impacting students.

References

American Speech Language Hearing Association. (n.d.). *States with restrictions on diversity, equity, and inclusion concepts in higher education.* Retrieved July 24, 2024, from https://www.asha.org/advocacy/state/state-mandates-around-diversity-equity-and-inclusion/states-with-restrictions-on-diversity-equity-and-inclusion-concepts-in-higher-education

Battle, S., & Wheeler, T. E. II. U.S. Department of Education. (2017). *Dear colleague: Title IX questions and answers* [PDF]. https://www.ed.gov/media/document/colleague-2017-title-ix-35085.pdf

Clinical and Translational Science Awards Consortium. (2011). *Principles of community engagement* (No. 508). https://stacks.cdc.gov/view/cdc/11699

Ford, S. (2021). Learning while black: How "Z learning while black: How "ZERO tolerance" policies disproportionately affect black students. *University of Florida Journal of Law & Public Policy, 32*(1), 49–70.

Garcetti v. Ceballos, No. 04-473 (Supreme Court of the United States May 30, 2006).

Lhamon, C., & Gupta, V. (2016). *Dear colleague letter on transgender students.* U.S. Department of Education and U.S. Department of Justice.

Love, B. L. (2023). *Punished for dreaming: How school reform harms black children and how we heal* (1st ed.). St. Martin's Press, an imprint of St. Martin's Publishing Group.

MindShift. (2016, October 2). *When schools take safety too far: The origins of zero-tolerance discipline*. KQED. https://www.kqed.org/mindshift/46517/when-schools-take-safety-too-far-the-origins-of-zero-tolerance-discipline

Movement Advancement Project. (n.d.). *Equality maps: LGBTQ curricular laws*. Retrieved July 15, 2024, from https://www.mapresearch.org/equality_maps/curricular_laws

Pelsue, B. (2017, August 29). When it comes to education, the federal government is in charge of ... um, what? *Harvard Ed*. https://www.gse.harvard.edu/ideas/ed-magazine/17/08/when-it-comes-education-federal-government-charge-um-what

Somander, T. (2014, September 23). *"The most important title is 'citizen'": President Obama on the significance of a civil society*. Obama White House. https://obamawhitehouse.archives.gov/blog/2014/09/23/most-important-title-citizen-president-obama-importance-civil-society

St. George, D. (2016, October 25). Resolution, years later, in boy's suspension over 'pastry gun.' *The Washington Post*. https://www.washingtonpost.com/local/education/resolution-years-later-in-boys-suspension-over-pastry-gun/2016/10/25/6bc337de-96f5-11e6-bc79-af1cd3d2984b_story.html

Trump White House Archives. (2020, December 28). Executive order on expanding educational opportunity through school choice. https://trumpwhitehouse.archives.gov/presidential-actions/executive-order-expanding-educational-opportunity-school-choice/

USA Facts. (2023, March 30). *Which states passed laws restricting school curriculum?* https://web.archive.org/web/20240616172833/https://usafacts.org/articles/which-states-passed-laws-restricting-school-curriculum/

U.S. Department of Education. (n.d.). White House *initiative on advancing educational equity, excellence, and economic opportunity* for *black* Americans. Retrieved July 12, 2024, from https://sites.ed.gov/whblackinitiative/executive-order/

3

BETTER UNDERSTAND YOUR SCHOOL

What kind of school do you work in? Examine the words you used to describe your school. Did you use the terms private, public, or charter? Did you say Title I? While schools could be described in any number of ways, we often fall back on descriptors that indicate funding and level of need. In the most generous analysis, we might be sharing our school makeup. In reality, we often use words like "Title I school" as code for students of color or low performing. In Chapter 2, we explored laws and policies; in this chapter, we will be taking a look at the system of educational institutions that impact how our students experience school.

Key Factors Outside the School Environment

Public School Funding

For our purposes, we will identify public schools as schools that are publicly funded and led by a democratically elected board of education with a school district. Public schools receive funding through federal, state, and local sources. Federal spending accounts for about 10% of funding for K-12 education (Hanson, 2024). State funding can vary widely. According to educationdata.org, in 2023, New York state spent $30,282 per student, while Idaho spent $8,748.

Local funding is typically dependent on property tax values. Districts with higher home values have more funding. Some districts are able to add additional property tax for the purpose of the school system. An NPR article notes that a poorer district in Illinois spends $9,794 per student, while an hour away, a different district spends $28,639 (Turner et al., 2016).

When considering income-dependent funding of schools, the intersections of race and poverty must be considered. The Center for American Progress found that schools with 90% students of color spent less money (or had less money) than schools with 90% white students (Spatig-Amerikaner, 2012).

In 1973 *San Antonio ISD v. Rodriguez*, the Supreme Court ruled that funding through property tax does not violate the equal protection clause of the 14th Amendment (*San Antonio Independent School District v. Rodriguez*, 1973). If this is how funding will continue for the foreseeable future, the impact of funding decisions is crucial to work related to equity in education.

Charter School Funding

Charter schools are public schools that have site-based decision-making. They receive funding from state and federal sources and, in some cases, directly from local districts on a per-pupil basis. Charter school laws and policies may vary from state to state. The idea is that charter schools are able to act more flexibly without the oversight of a school board, district policies, etc. Some charter schools are managed by for-profit companies.

When charters are managed by for-profit companies or by individuals who see them as an entrepreneurial opportunity, there is an incentive to recruit students who are less likely to be homeless, need an Individualized Education Plan (IEP), or have behavioral challenges (Douglass Horsford et al., 2019). I know in my state, North Carolina, charter schools are required to accept all students but anecdotally we hear that they persuade parents to send their children with greater needs back to public districts rather than work through challenges.

In reality, charter schools come with a variety of strengths and concerning trends. While some data suggest that charter schools outperform traditional public schools to some extent, other data are inconclusive. In North Carolina, 23 charter schools closed without ever opening, pulling funds from local education agencies with no services provided to students (North Carolina Department of Public Instruction, 2023). In North Carolina, local school district budgets include a line for payment to charter schools depending on their enrollment.

The reverse side of the flexibility that charters offer is that they are not required to provide the same level of services as public schools, for example, transportation or free and reduced lunch. This allows charter schools to select certain students and turn others away because of a "lack of programming."

Central Office

In public school systems, central offices lead the work of the school through guidance, organization, and funding. School systems vary widely in size – from less than 100 students to the NYC Department of Education with 1.1 million. Of course, most districts are somewhere in between. When the central office becomes too large, it can take money away from programs that impact the student experience. On the other side, without central office support, either because the district is too small, it's a charter school, or there isn't support for the type of role that an educator holds, there is no external thought partner for the building staff. This can lead to stagnation and feelings of isolation. In addition, work supported by central office will fall on school-based employees including mandated federal and state reporting, data disaggregation, and other important tasks.

Central office can be overspecialized, meaning that positions are so specialized that they don't encompass the full work of educating students. In a district where I worked, there were coaches for core, intervention, ELA, math, behavior, and the list goes on. This often caused confusion for school staff on who to call. The departments sometimes disagreed on how the workflow should be handled. When there is overspecialization, each specialty may only consider the best way to handle their content without considering the importance of other areas. For example, if all four core content areas give the guidance that their content should be taught for 2 hours each, the school can't align with all of the guidance it received. This is a simple example, but one that I see played out over and over.

School Assignment

It can be argued that school assignment is the crux of inequality in public education. After all, where a student goes to school determines their educational experience and influences all academic outcomes. In April 2024, nonpartisan education watchdog group Available to All released a study "The Broken Promise of Brown v Board of Ed" (2024).

The study finds that all 50 states and the District of Columbia allow school assignment to be connected to a student's address. Combined with the long history of housing discrimination in the United States, school zones based on address de facto segregate students by race. "The Broken Promise" report calls this "educational redlining" where the attendance zones of many desirable public schools mirror the patterns of redlining maps (Available to All, 2024, p. 1)

Connect segregated educational redlining with school funding based on property taxes and we can quickly see that schools in predominantly Black and brown neighborhoods are often underfunded and under-resourced. "The Broken Promise" report shares the story of two schools in the Old Town neighborhood in Chicago. At one school, 84% of eighth graders can read proficiently. Just 1 mile away, not one eighth grader can read proficiently. Of course, not all students who want to can attend the higher achieving school, there are only so many seats. But what is not happening is an equal opportunity to access to enroll. The report finds that families have weak legal protections when it comes to access to specific schools, discrimination in admissions is often allowed or even required by law, and significant inconsistencies or loopholes exist that allow school leaders to control the makeup of the school.

High-stakes testing incentivizes school leaders to prioritize school assignment that benefits their school. If a high school was looking at students who enroll in their school, are they more likely to prefer students from the school with no proficient readers or the school with 84% proficiency? Free Appropriate Public Education (FAPE) is supposed to be for all but this is not always the case. Once students are in the building, many factors *within* the school impact a student's educational experience.

Key Factors Within the School Environment

The real difficulty in changing the course of any enterprise lies not in developing new ideas, but in escaping old ones.

~John Maynard Keynes (Western Australian Agriculture Authority, 2017)

Administration

Public schools are typically led by a principal, perhaps with the support of assistant principal(s), under the supervision of a central office and, ultimately, the school board. In some charter or private schools, decisions may be made by a CEO or board. Depending on the governing body, the purpose of the charter school may be profit. However, decisions on practices (rather than policies or laws), are often led by the principal even if designed by the central office or board. Principals have many responsibilities and are often overwhelmed by the amount of information that is expected to flow through their leadership. During the COVID-19 pandemic, a gif circulated where a person is hit over and over by a large ball that keeps knocking them down, titled "Principals during COVID-19." I think about this gif often when considering frustrations related to building leaders' implementation of good practices for student outcomes.

The leadership style of the principal will impact change-making within the building. A study of principal leadership styles and their relationship to student achievement (in one course) found that the democratic leadership style led to better student outcomes (Achimungu & Phebe Obaka, 2019). If you are not the principal, you don't have much influence over the administrator's leadership style. Looking at three major leadership styles: authoritarian, laissez-faire, and democratic, how can we impact change in the environment of that building?

In an authoritarian leadership style, the leader focuses on dominating and often does not delegate responsibilities. This can lead to staff feeling angry, unheard, or frustrated. Staff who feel negatively will be less likely to engage in the creative, student-affirming teaching that we want for all students. This type of leadership style might also be less welcoming to ideas related to equity for all student groups if this was not already an important factor for them.

Make It Work:

- Connect your work to their work. Think about what's important to your leader and make sure that what you are working on is connected to their very important projects.
- Make suggestions and not demands. Being assertive is important but you know your environment best. If that's not likely to go well, consider other, softer routes for sharing your ideas.
- Ask in a group. The more staff who work together to create change, the more support you may get from your leadership. But be thoughtful, in a true authoritarian style this may be seen as unacceptable dissent.

In a laissez-faire leadership style, all responsibilities are given to subordinates. Staff and students alike are free to do as they please. This might seem nice but can result in disorganization, lack of direction, and unclear processes and procedures.

Make It Work:

- Work in committees. With the lack of direction from leadership, teachers, counselors, and educators can work together in committees to create structures that impact change.
- Take concerns to the "doers." Schools wouldn't function without "doers" – these are the folks that are making sure the school keeps running. You know who these people are.
- Keep the big picture in mind. Some laissez-faire leaders are happy to go along with ideas as long as it's clear what the plan is. Present ideas as they are fully developed and don't wait for the plan to come from the leader. With a clear vision, they may give you their full support.

In a democratic leadership style, active participation of subordinates is encouraged in decision-making. Teachers, students, and families are likely to feel engaged in the process of decision-making and are motivated and creative. This improves the school's goals and, ultimately, the achievement of students.

Make It Work:

- Recognize it might take longer. When a leader encourages active participation from all groups, decision-making may take longer but will be more robust and effective in the end.
- Follow the process. Democratic leaders typically have ways that they seek input; align with that process as much as possible so that your work doesn't derail the work that's been done.
- Speak out often. If your leader is asking for your voice and opinion, give it! Use this opportunity to work toward change.

Educators

In the 2020–2021 school year, 80% of teachers were white, while 46% of students were white (National Center for Education Statistics, 2023). Educator diversity has long been an issue post-Brown when large numbers of teachers lost their jobs with the integration of schools but with the rising shortage of teachers, it will likely get worse. Racial and ethnic diversity benefits all students. Students of color benefit from having teachers of color both academically and with reduced disciplinary issues (Greenberg Motamedi & Stevens, 2018). White students also benefit from having teachers of color through exposure to multiple perspectives and an increase in their ability to solve problems and think critically.

The Regional Education Laboratory published a set of materials on how to expand human resources practices to result in the hiring and retention of educators of color (Greenberg Motamedi & Stevens, 2018). Their recommendations include strategies in recruiting, selecting and hiring, and onboarding and recruiting. From posting positions early to broaden the net for potential candidates, to expanding beyond the use of personal networks of current staff, and then high-quality onboarding and support, schools can use low-cost evidence-based practices to not only hire diverse educators but to help them stay in the profession and in the school.

Educators in the building also include access to support staff. Schools in lower income areas and schools with higher percentages of students of color are likely to have less access to support staff like counselors, librarians, and school nurses. In a landmark ruling in North Carolina,

Leandro v. The State of North Carolina, federal courts ruled that the state must provide equal opportunity for a sound education to all. In 2019, I participated in a panel with the state's Leandro Commission to hear about the shortage of "specialized instructional support personnel." In this session, the commission explored the shortage of school counselors, school social workers, school psychologists, and school nurses in districts across the state. Not surprisingly, low-income areas of North Carolina were more directly affected.

Low-income schools are also more likely to lack a school librarian. In Philadelphia, the district employs only four full-time certified librarians (D'Onofrio, 2024). The SLIDE project for school librarians found that equity differences in access to librarians are associated with race, ethnicity, and poverty. Students of color have less access to school librarians (SLIDE Press Release, 2023).

Access to this type of support staff is crucial for the support of students as a whole child with interests, difficulties, strengths, and weaknesses. Intersectionality of race and poverty combined with the trauma associated with racism means that students of color need this access. A brief by the Learning Policy Institute found that Black students attending high-poverty schools have less access than white students attending high-poverty schools. The brief states: "Students at these schools endure cumulative disadvantage from inadequate and unequal resources and opportunities at school and from the failure of schools to address adverse out-of-school conditions that inhibit learning and development" (Oakes et al., 2021).

Student Body

Discussions around the student body of a school often center around a deficit-based mindset. To counter that, let's explore the concept of Community Cultural Wealth and consider whether schools can more effectively capitalize on this cultural wealth in the support of student learning. Yosso's Cultural Wealth model includes six forms of cultural capital, we will explore each of the six areas and consider how schools can take advantage of the cultural wealth of the students and families to maximize positive outcomes for students and, perhaps most importantly, to increase a positive school environment for staff and students (Yosso, 2005).

Aspirational Capital

The ability to maintain hope and dreams for the future in the face of real and perceived barriers. In schools, this is often an aspiration for education. It might be because of financial mobility or simply the idea that education is a means to improve your life outcomes. In schools, this means that families have Big Dreams for their children. They can acknowledge the hardships that might be along the way but they have goals.

Honoring Aspirational Capital:
- Ask (really ask!) students and families about their goals.
- Have realistic and honest conversations about how the school can help the student reach those goals.
- Remain positive – don't squash a student or family's aspirations based on your opinion of the likelihood of success.
- Check in often – how is the student progressing toward the goal? What does the student or family need to make better progress?

Linguistic Capital

Intellectual and social skills attained through communication experiences in more than one language and/or style. Students of color arrive at school with multiple language and communication skills. Perhaps they are bilingual and translate for family members, or have a rich history of storytelling traditions, they may be adept at communicating via visual art, music, or poetry. Students with linguistic capital are aware of their audience, including cross-cultural awareness, real-world literacy skills, and a sense of civic and familial responsibility.

Honoring Linguistic Capital:
- Actively encourage students and families to speak the language of their choosing in the school setting.
- Provide and successfully utilize interpreters.
- Give voice and choice to students on how they share their learning, including ways that amplify their linguistic capital.

Familial Capital

A common sense of community history, memory, and cultural intuition. In this capital, there is a commitment to community well-being with an importance on maintaining healthy connections to our community and its resources. This community is also a model for positive characteristics that inform the emotional, moral, and educational consciousness.

Honoring Familial Capital:

- Create opportunities for students to recognize the wisdom, values, and stories from their home communities.
- Invite the whole family! Ensure adequate space and time for extended family members to be present and a part of the school.
- Be respectful of religious and cultural differences while allowing time and space for students to see themselves reflected in their learning.

Social Capital

The networks of people and community resources. This type of network can increase opportunities for students and add to the emotional support they feel in reaching their aspirations. There is a long history of mutual aid societies that "lift as we climb" in order to support individuals within a system that is working against them (Yosso, 2005).

Honoring Social Capital:

- When working with families, ask about their social networks and supports within their community. Don't assume they have none.
- Work with students to stay connected to the communities and individuals who are supportive of their success. Ask students who that is to them.
- Engage with community resources to welcome their work in collaboration with the school.

Navigational Capital

The skill and ability to navigate social institutions including educational spaces. People of Color must use this capital to navigate complex systems that were not created with communities of color in mind. It connects the social network to the navigation of systems such as college, PreK-12 schooling, job market, and the health care system.

Honoring Navigational Capital:
- Ask what systems are difficult to navigate in the school setting and work *with* families to change them.
- Increase transparency of processes and procedures to lower the access point in the school.
- Work with families to increase the navigational capital for all, especially in areas where the school has little control such as food access, library resources, and social services.

Resistant Capital

The knowledge and skills fostered through oppositional behavior that challenges inequity. While it might feel like this type of capital is the school's adversary, this set of skills can be your greatest advocate for all students.

Honoring Resistant Capital:
- Identify parents and families with resistant capital and invite them to be a part of decision-making groups within the school.
- Share information on factors outside of the building that are impacting the work of the school and ask for help in influencing change.
- Amplify the voice of students with resistant capital by giving them space to share their advocacy work and connect with other students who might have similar interests.

PTA and Foundations

We would be remiss to talk about factors within a school building without discussing Parent Teacher Associations (PTAs) and foundations that supplement the spending of schools. Spending by these organizations disproportionately goes to wealthier and whiter schools. One school near me has a foundation with an annual budget of $250,000. This entire sum goes to one school in addition to the budget they receive from the district. The school where I worked for years is 5 miles away and for many years had no PTA at all. A current search could not find a budget for the PTA at that school. PTAs could go well beyond this amount and there is little oversight or rules related to their spending. Almost all PTA funding is by school rather than by district and creates further opportunity gaps for education between high-income and low-income schools.

There is no way for us to know every aspect of every school. We've given you some key areas where we see disparities between educational opportunities, both through factors outside the building and factors within. Through your self-work, collaborative work, and professional learning work, your task is to determine changes that are needed for your specific building, district, or state. If we all work against the status quo, in the places we are, we can see greater changes as a whole.

Do what you can, with what you've got, where you are.

Although this quote is widely attributed to Theodore Roosevelt, he credits it, in his *Autobiography*, Chapter IX, to Squire Bill Widener of Widener's Valley, Virginia (Theodore Roosevelt Center, n.d.).

Doing the Work

In each Doing the Work section, we will take the learning from the chapter and apply it to self-work, collaborative work, and professional learning work. To impact change, we must do the work.

Self-Work

Self-work in equity spaces begins with self-reflection. When considering the external and internal factors that impact your building, many of which disproportionately negatively impact students of color, you may be disgusted and want to walk away from that school or even the field of education. You may be disgusted and want to stay. Neither is wrong. I believe that in order to impact change, systems must have forces outside who are disrupting and forces inside that are working to change the system. We often characterize Diversity Equity and Inclusion (DEI) work as disrupting the system, and while that is true, no member of the system can disrupt as much as a person outside of the system – they'd be fired. It takes both.

I once worked at a school where I was appalled by inequitable practices from the beginning. I was determined to be a part of the change. I worked hard to create change in that school but continuously butted up against the administrator and other political forces. Finally, I began to feel like I was a part of the problem rather than a coconspirator for change. I decided to leave. I struggled with that decision. While my leaving might be the right thing to do overall (and for me), what did that mean for the students who were there? I had to reflect and recognize that my work was needed elsewhere and that perhaps another educator who came after me would be able to make better headway for change.

> What aspects of your current role don't sit right with you? Where do you feel a disconnect from what is right for students and what you are doing?

If you can't find any examples of how your current role doesn't sit well or where there is no cognitive dissonance for your role and the role of equity interrupter, I urge you to reconsider. Considering the current state of our education system, it seems almost impossible to find a situation where all is well. Consider asking those around you what is working well and what continues to need work, where students and families, maybe even colleagues, are being marginalized. Watch and observe, listen to understand. Once you have determined a few (or maybe many) of your hot points for change, you are ready to move on to the next step.

> What have you already done to create change within your school to decrease the predictability of success or failure that correlates with race, disability, or socioeconomic status?

> What have you already done to create change outside of your school to decrease the predictability of success or failure that correlates with race, disability, or socioeconomic status?

> What areas of learning do you still need to explore?

Action:

- Determine an area where you will interrupt the status quo. Consider who the changemakers are that you need to work with to make that happen.
- Write down two action steps that you will take to make a change toward decreasing the predictability of success or failure of students.

Collaborative Work

In the book, *Street Data*, authors Safir and Dugan explore school transformation through a different lens (Safir, 2021). One of their main tenets is to "center voices from the margin." In order to do this as a practitioner, they share several strategies that we'll highlight here.

Demographic scan: Take a look at different types of classes on your campus – can you tell which class you are looking at by noting demographic make-ups?

What is the current landscape of equity at our school?

What is happening to cause this pattern?

How many of the items that you noted are based on the learner and assumptions (or even knowledge of) their skills, home life, extracurricular activities, or attitude about school?

How many of the items you noted are based on the instruction, curriculum, or environment of the class?

How can you decenter the focus on learner deficits to consider changes in instruction, curriculum, or environment?

Listening campaigns: Check in with students whose voices are not typically heard and ask how the experience of school is for them. Select a listener who can organize what is shared into anonymous quotes for leadership teams, administrators, and teachers. Be broad and open with questions asked and choose about five students so that you can notice patterns in what is shared.

For the adult listener, how honest do you think the students were in what they shared? What is your sense of the trust that they felt in the conversation? If a student were to disagree with you on that assessment, what do you think they would say?

What patterns do you notice in what students shared?

What patterns did you notice in what students did not share?

Now that you've heard from students, what follow-up questions would you have? How might you find the answers to these questions?

Action:

- Add listening opportunities with students, families, and colleagues throughout your day.
- Start to take note when you hear yourself or colleagues share concerns that are based on learner attributes or assumptions rather than instruction, curriculum, or environment.
- Challenge yourself to share one instruction, curriculum, or environment example in all data-based problem-solving teams.

Professional Learning Work

In this chapter, we have reviewed the impacts, push and pulls factors, and considered the power dynamics of working and leading a school. One of the areas that we haven't considered is how equity work happens in your building. *Street Data* explores a number of "traps and tropes" for equity work. For example, does your school bring in experts but with no ongoing plan for learning or capacity building? Authors Safir and Dugan (2021) call this "Spray and Pray Equity." Do your conversations involve lots of self-reflection but no action steps? This is "Navel-gazing Equity."

How do conversations about equity go in your building? What goes well? What could benefit from change?

How does your school use data when discussing equity?

Does your school purposefully seek the voices of the marginalized in your community?

Does your school respond to the "squeakiest wheel," sometimes at the expense of others?

Recently, I have seen an image being shared relating to inequality, equality, equity, and justice (Ruth, 2019). It is reminiscent of The Giving Tree and depicts two little boys seeking apples.

- Inequality image: One boy gets apples and the other doesn't. The writing says, "unequal access to opportunities." The boy with no apples has a question mark above his head.
- Equality image: Both boys have ladders and bags. The writing says, "Evenly distributed tools and assistance." However, one boy's ladder isn't tall enough for his side of the tree and he has an exclamation point above his head (no apples).
- Equity image: Both boys have ladders and bags. Both of their ladders are tall enough. The writing says, "Custom tools that identify and address inequality." One ladder is taller than the other, both boys have apples but one boy's side of the tree has less apples on it.
- Justice Image: Both boys have ladders and bags. The writing says, "Fixing the system to offer equal access to both tools and opportunities." In this image, the tree has support structures so that both sides are at the same height and have the same number of apples.

When you read these descriptions, which one most reminds you of your school?

What would your school look like if there was justice?

What actions would it take **outside** of your school to make that justice happen?

What actions would it take **inside** your school to make that justice happen?

What actions would it take **from you** to make that justice happen?

Action:

- Create an equity team – a group of colleagues, either formal or informal, that is committed to working together to make your school a better place for all learners and their families.
- Take the time to dig deep into the data for your own work within your building and for the school as a whole. What disparities do you see? Consider possible causes that don't include learner deficits.
- Work with others in your building to seek the input from parents, families, and staff members who might have less opportunity to share their thoughts on all aspects of the school. Carefully consider making sure that space is a safe space for participants

References

Achimungu, L., & Phebe Obaka, H. (2019). Influence of principals' leadership styles on senior secondary school students' achievement in chemistry. *Science Education International, 30*(2), 92–96.

Available to All. (2024). *The Broken Promise of Brown v Board of Ed: A 50-state report on legal discrimination in public school admissions.* https://availabletoall.org/wp-content/uploads/2024/04/ata-brownvbofed.full4_.23.24.pdf

D'Onofrio, M. (2024, March 27). *Most Philadelphia district schools lack librarians.* Axios Philadelphia. https://www.axios.com/local/philadelphia/2024/03/27/school-district-libraries-missing-librarians

Douglass Horsford, S., Scott, J. T., & Anderson, G. L. (2019). *The politics of education policy in an era of inequality* (Educational leadership for equity and diversity series). Routledge.

Greenberg Motamedi, J., & Stevens, D. (2018, November 6). *Human resources practices for recruiting, selecting, and retaining teachers of color*. Washington State Vibrant Teaching Force Alliance. https://ies.ed.gov/ncee/edlabs/regions/northwest/pdf/human-resources-practices.pdf

Hanson, M. (2024, July 14). *U.S. public education spending statistics*. https://educationdata.org/public-education-spending-statistics

National Center for Education Statistics. (2023). *Characteristics of public school teachers (condition of education)*. U.S. Department of Education, Institute of Education Sciences. https://nces.ed.gov/programs/coe/indicator/clr

North Carolina Department of Public Instruction. (2023). Highlights of the North Carolina *public school budget. https://www.dpi.nc.gov/documents/fbs/resources/2023-highlightspdf/download?attachment*

Oakes, J., Cooks, P. W. Jr., George, J., Levin, S., Carver-Thomas, D., Frelow, F., & Berry, B. (2021). *Adequate and equitable education in high-poverty schools: Barriers and opportunities in North Carolina*. Learning Policy Institute. https://learningpolicyinstitute.org/product/leandro-high-poverty-schools-brief

Ruth, T. (2019). *Equality, equity and justice* [graphic]. https://www.researchgate.net/figure/Equality-Equity-and-Justice-Source-Tony-Ruth-from-Maeda-2019_fig2_354087577

Safir, S. & Dugan, J. (2021). *Street data: A next-generation model for equity, pedagogy, and school transformation* (1st ed). SAGE Publications.

San Antonio Independent School District v. Rodriguez, No. No. 71-1332 (U.S. Supreme Court March 21, 1973).

SLIDE Press Release. (2023, August 31). Schools *without libraries*: First *school level data on the po*st-COVID *era*. https://libslide.org/news/june-15th-press-release/

Spatig-Amerikaner, A. (2012). *Unequal education: Federal loophole enables lower spending on students of color (progress 2050)*. Center for American Progress.

Theodore Roosevelt Center. (n.d.). Theodore Roosevelt *quotes*. Retrieved August 22, 2024, from https://www.theodorerooseveltcenter.org/Learn-About-TR/TR-Quotes

Turner, C., Khrais, R., Lloyd, T., Olgin, A., Isensee, L., Vevea, B., & Carsen, D. (2016, April 18). *Why America's schools have a money problem*. Npr.Org. https://www.npr.org/2016/04/18/474256366/why-americas-schools-have-a-money-problem

Western Australian Agriculture Authority. (2017). *Planning systems, continuity, innovation and change (plan, prepare, prosper)*. https://www.agric.wa.gov.au/sites/gateway/files/7.2%20Systems%20Continuity%20Innovation%20and%20Change%20-%20Work%20Book.pdf

Yosso, T. J. (2005). Whose culture has capital? A critical race theory discussion of community cultural wealth. *Race Ethnicity and Education*, *8*(1), 69–91.

4

YOU AND YOUR SCHOOL COMMUNITY
INTENSIVE SELF-REFLECTION

In her book *Teaching to Transgress*, author and educator bell hooks (1994) (intentionally lowercase) calls on the lessons of monk and peace activist, Thich Nhat Hanh who noted how the practice of educators must look inward in hopes of helping others.

In this chapter, we are extending this idea to all types of educators. As we relate to ourselves and each other, so must we relate to our students and their families despite similarities and differences. Whether our differences be cultural, racial, socioeconomic, gender, political, or ethnic, we give to others what we have been given and that we have given to ourselves.

Organizations like schools are made up of people, and people bring their beliefs, behaviors, biases, prejudices, wisdom, etc. to organizations. Likewise, organizations impact people's way of thinking and being. Have you ever witnessed a colleague's positive impact on a school community? Have you ever observed an unhealthy coworker leave a negative mark on others? **Harm can happen in schools as much as healing can happen in schools.** What we bring to the school community can shift the culture in one direction or another or anywhere between extremes. For all of the exercises and questions in this chapter, we can effectively swap out teachers for administrators, school counselors, school psychologists, paraprofessionals, or anyone who is an adult in a school building. The influences

DOI: 10.4324/9781003423126-4

of individuals who hold power within a school have lasting effects on that system and other educational institutions, processes, and practices. We must not dismiss or ignore the power various people hold within our schools and districts because they too have perspectives, lived experiences, perceptions, and beliefs that will impact their leadership and decisions. What impact might an engaged, self-aware, self-reflective, flexible, and personally accountable leader have on a building?

Self-exploration can bridge the autopilot of old habits and the realization of personal and professional goals. Additionally, we must self-examine our relationship to our visible and invisible identities and consequently to students and other educators. Throughout this text, we don't shy away from noticing the impact of marginalization within the educational system. Because our identities and experiences dictate so much of the educational process throughout the country, we must attend to how it impacts our ability to be honest about our own history, perceptions, and practice.

Embrace Complexity

Nonbinary thinking refers to how we understand ourselves and the world beyond good or bad, nice or mean, qualified or unqualified, and capable or incapable. When two opposing ideas seem always opposing, they may be considered binary: off and on, up or down, etc. When two ideas seem to be the only two options, this is also a binary, such as whether a student is high-achieving or not. But we know as practitioners that this is rarely true because the human condition is incredibly complex and dependent on many factors. In education, it is essential that we embrace complex and critical thinking so that we can appreciate the nuance of humankind and honor how our individual and collective histories have shaped our present-day understanding. The reality of education means that educators at all grade levels can think in complex ways that don't have to feel overwhelming or confusing so that we can be effective in our professional and personal lives. Most of us do this anyway. Most of us do this now. Accepting that life is complex can be pivotal in engaging with the rest of this chapter. Readers will be tasked to untangle experiences and critically think through problem-solving. Collaborating with a trusted partner while reading may also be beneficial.

Self-Exploration

While this text is not a self-help book, the ongoing self-work necessary for all people to explore in this chapter might be a vital step toward embracing systemic change. **It starts with you.** Some educators maintain professional educator supervision or personal therapy as one option that helps start the change process. Ongoing self-exploration is a part of, if not critical to, systemic change. Organizations operate as external structures with histories and policies, while those who make up that system maintain the status quo. For example, have you been told to keep your personal life separate from your professional life? What does that mean? Does that mean you are a different person at home than at work? How does this impact the way your school is governed? Or are you the same person in thoughts and behavior across all scenarios in your life, including work and home? Without self-judgment, consider what it means to be one personality in one setting and a different personality in another. Might you be the same person in all settings but access various and diverse sets of skills in differing environments? Often, our worlds of personal and professional overlap and it is difficult to compartmentalize, siloing versions of ourselves in specific scenarios. Spend a moment thinking about why your school environment calls for this. Can you authentically be selfless at work and selfish at home? Is that how you want to be? Are there consequences for being the same in your personal and professional life? For many educators, being different in different scenarios depends on the circumstance, the day, and the self-awareness. How much of yourself do you bring to your work? Your personality? Your life experiences? Is it realistic or even possible to be a different person in your job than in your home? How and why? Are you active in the political scene in your community but attempt to remain "neutral" while at work? Is this required of you? The answers and discussions derived from these questions can shed light on what your school environment requires and expects of people. Challenging and questioning the nature of who you are and where you are authentic can help you identify where to begin or continue self-work within the context of education. Remember to show yourself compassion and get support through these exercises.

Flexibility and Nuance

What we offer in this chapter is a theme of flexibility and nuance. Educators who feel compelled to be consistently authoritarian with students but conversely permissive in their personal lives may benefit from exploring that difference. Is there a difference, and why? What makes your students different from your own children or your nieces and nephews? Have you considered the consequences of refusing the status quo at your school or community? Have you witnessed others reject or dismantle the status quo at your school? What happened? The objective here is to embrace continued self-discovery as you relate to your loved ones, students, and colleagues. You are as much a part of your institution's system as anyone else in the building. Who you are helps shape the system. Who your colleagues are helps shape the system, too. How we interact with the system establishes school culture, climate, practices, and routines. These routines become embedded and shift depending on everyone in the school community.

"Educators' ability to reflect, deconstruct, and redesign routines should be prominent in our school improvement practice" (Diamond & Gomez, 2023, p. 7). Habitualizing these reflection routines must be a priority of administration and districts. The skills required to self-reflect can be honed with questioning, discussion, workshopping, co-planning, codesigning, and journaling. Often professional development time at the beginning of the school year and at the end of the school does not allow for dedicated self-reflection. It must. Maintaining structured ways to reflect upon our personal and professional growth is imperative. Ignoring our impact on our school communities is a disservice to students and their families. Better understanding our routines, procedures, and how we engage our roles can make the difference between dismantling harmful practices and creating healing learning spaces. Get to know what roles you play.

Know Your Role

Who you are tasked to be within your school community may impact your approach to self-discovery. Often, leaders believe they are responsible for being in charge of everyone in the building. Consider these questions to discuss with a thought partner:

What do you believe an effective leader does?

Do they finalize decisions?

Do they ensure employees are following the rules?

Do they listen to students and incorporate the feedback of others?

In what ways do leaders embrace their own self-discovery?

Is the self-discovery of leaders personal and hidden or transparent and openly discussed?

Who leads in your school? The principal? Teachers? The school counselor? Students?

Do you believe some people make better leaders than others?

Do you notice a pattern of who becomes a leader in your district? To what do you attribute this pattern?

In the previous chapter, we learned about the school system's structure and school building. What do you make of that structure? Is it fair and just, or do you notice certain groups of people holding power in your school system?

Is it a structure that works for all the people within your community? Why or why not, and what role do you play in that?

Often, we learn hierarchical views of leadership where one person is in charge and one person disperses policy and practices "downward." Not all school leaders function in this manner, but many do, and as part of better understanding our relationships to leadership we should reveal our thoughts and ideas about leadership. Ultimately, this will help us better understand how we function within the system, given the roles we are assigned and the roles we assume.

In the previous chapters, we learned about three styles of leadership:

1. Authoritarian-style leaders
2. Laissez-fair leaders
3. Democratic leaders

Without judgment about which type of leader you tend to be, take inventory of what life events may have contributed to where you find yourself today as a leader and educator. Do you attribute your style to your personality, being the firstborn, being a Leo, or being from the city? Maybe it's related to something else you've identified earlier in your life such as a mentor or a middle school leadership experience. Who were the leaders early in your life, and what were they like? When completing my internship at two different public schools in Philadelphia, I was greatly influenced by the Latina women who supervised me. They taught me about bringing my whole self to education and the sociocultural influences I did not learn from my graduate schooling. Coincidentally, it was a Latina professor in graduate school who shed light on the women of color voices often excluded from academia. These were voices I needed to hear and learn from as I studied and interned to become an educator decades ago. Without placing value or judgment on the factors that contributed to your present style, use this moment in the text to embrace the factors that led to you being you. All of it was real, for better or worse, and discovering what has impacted your worldview will assist you in making more intentional decisions about how you plan to move forward, using the worldview you cultivate from this moment. You are more than a product of your lived experiences. You get to choose what kind of person you want to be.

Consider the nuances and areas of flexibility within your leadership or educator style. This book may use leader and educator interchangeably throughout each chapter. Does your role shift given a specific circumstance or group of people with whom you interact? Why do you think this is? Again, we hope in this self-exploration you will notice the complexity of your leadership skills and style even if you don't consider yourself to be a leader in a traditional sense. Your style may even include multiple leadership types or none listed. You lead the classroom, or you may lead discussions or counseling groups. You may notice how receptive to your style some are, while others aren't. Flexibility can offer you different access points should you be self-aware and insightful enough to gauge when you need to be flexible. Flexibility is where we allow ourselves and others to think beyond binaries of good or bad, right or wrong, and embrace "sometimes good enough" or "presently not strong in this area but working on developing this skill." Have you ever realized in the moment as you work with a student that your approach to them is not as effective as the same approach with another student? Don't take these instances for granted. This is a moment where you "read the room," relying on your intuition and experience and trusting a more flexible stance. These skills can be honed, taught, and sharpened over time to help us be more self-aware practitioners and more in-tuned human beings. Many of us learned this out of necessity during the earliest days of the 2020 global COVID pandemic. As many schools closed and shifted to virtual learning, educators and administrators quickly adapted to more flexible ways of teaching and educating. Colleges adapted more flexible policies to continue admitting qualified students without standardized test scores or passing grades instead of letter or numerical grades. Traditionally in-person schools relied on the wisdom of their colleagues at cyberschools. As leaders, we adjusted. We need to continue to adjust to create better systems. So, consider the role you play and why you play that role. Who you are matters when adjusting to being more intentional as a practitioner and simply as a person. How you relate to the world around you shows up in your educator and leadership style. As difficulty emerges and systems seek change, a self-reflective educator is a prepared educator, and you'll have the tools you need to weather many storms.

Power and Authority

As we know, the largest group of people within a school is the student body. Teachers are often the second largest group of people within a school, and teachers have clearly defined roles as adults who teach content. Sometimes, content is aligned with social-emotional learning, and often, the content is dictated by the district and the state. It is worth further identifying teachers as leaders, not simply those who provide instruction. Remember, we remain flexible and nuanced in our approach to systemic change.

This includes adjusting our perceptions and being open to the possibility that our ideas about people and their roles can be more expansive. Every role as a leader in a school is worth exploring, including students, which we will discuss later. Whether these ideas are new to you or not, consider how your leadership as a teacher, specifically, contributes to the benefit of all students. If you are not a teacher, consider how the teachers in your school contribute to the benefit of all students. Teachers hold power. This is a complex idea because teachers are often underpaid in certain states and are not included in district-level decision-making. Systems make it difficult for teachers, counselors, paraprofessionals, and social workers to be as effective as they desire. Douglass-Horsford et al. (2019) tell us that over time and based on political leanings, teacher certification goals shift over time to meet the demands of what the political party deems necessary, not what teachers deem necessary based on the realities of their classrooms.

Most teachers will tell anyone willing to listen, that despite being with students every weekday for most of the day, they are not the primary decision-makers in their school or district. As instructors and assigned authorities in the classroom, teachers are generally the experts in the room, given their content area. They are leaders in their classroom, designating seating arrangements, unit plans, and sometimes materials for how their students will learn throughout the school year. There is often some choice as to how a teacher can approach a lesson, but evaluations of teachers may lead to more stringent fidelity to an assigned curriculum. Teachers may be culturally responsive or not; they may share aspects of their personal lives or aim to be "neutral." Whatever their approach, this often sets the tone within the classroom and ripples throughout the school. When this goes against what teachers believe is right or just, feelings of burnout and fatigue may surface.

Now, think about yourself as a teacher or keep a teacher's image in your mind:

What leadership qualities do you attribute to yourself or that teacher?

What makes them effective?

What is their personality like?

How do students respond to them?

If you are wondering this for yourself, write down or discuss the leadership qualities you exude in the classroom with a thought partner. What works? What doesn't work and why?

In your own schooling experience, what characteristics about your teachers worked for you?

How did your favorite or most well-respected teachers show up in class?

What did they do or say?

Did this align with what the school or district required of educators? How so?

Were there areas of misalignment? How did that impact the educator, students, and school community?

Most importantly, how did the teachers in your life use their power and authority?

Let's pause here and reflect on power and authority. There are social media posts and daily overheard conversations about teachers indoctrinating students or discouraging students from their aspirations. Let's honor these experiences by leaning into those conversations and not shying away from people's accounts of their educational journeys. Focusing on the positive experiences of teaching has a place in every discourse and the ills of our profession must also require some attention. Teachers are the educators with students most of the school day. How we show up in the classroom is interpreted as many times as there are students; this is to say that if you have 57 students to teach on a given day, you may be perceived 57 different ways. That's okay. That's honest and realistic. Are you able to be honest with yourself, and are your students able to be honest with you about how they perceive your power and authority in the classroom? If a student told you that they feel harmed by you, would you accept their truth? Or would you dismiss it away? Is this also true for you in your personal life?

Making It Work:

- Journal! If hearing feedback from students is difficult for you as an educator, practice exploring your thoughts and ideas. Describe the scenario from your perspective AND your student's perspective. What happened, and how did you respond? What contributed to you responding in this way? How might you respond differently in the future, and why?
- Adjust your flexibility. Do you feel you have to be the same type of person all the time with no room for humility or growth? This is an unhealthy state. As human beings, we are designed to learn and grow, which often means challenge and discomfort. Explore how you handle discomfort.
- Are you on autopilot? Have you been an educator or administrator for so long that you simply don't stop to self-reflect? How is that impacting you as a person and professional?
- What examples of power and authority existed throughout your life? Who did you believe was powerful or an authority, and why? Do these examples still work for you today?

Trauma-Informed Educating

This isn't just about students. This is also about your personal history and who it was shaped by. Maybe your own lived experiences are so far in the past that you don't consider them regularly. This is not meant to be therapeutic but possibly a pathway toward healing. Seek out treatment if you need it and get support to feel through these questions and insights. In Dr. Mullan's (2023) book *Decolonizing Therapy*, an acknowledgment is made of how war, poverty, epidemics, displacements, and other events impact individuals and communities. Educators are not exempt from feeling the effects of what happens globally. Time doesn't necessarily heal all wounds; we may need to attend to what plagues us outside of school to be more effective in our relationships in school.

Most American educators were raised and educated within this American educational system, particularly the adults who are now in charge of this system. It is one of the few characteristics most people have in common: we went to school. Given these common experiences, adjusting, re-routing, and dismantling the system may seem like an impossible feat, but change is inevitable. Change has always occurred. Change is the only guarantee. What type of change occurs remains to be determined and influenced by what is done today. We can repeat the dangers and injustices of the past, whether personally and/or professionally. Because educators and leaders remain unhealed, lacking self-reflection and self-awareness, injustices are maintained in different forms as change occurs.

Sustainability

We are asking educators to create schools they may have never seen.

Test scores, graduation rates, and college attainment often determine educational success. Without discounting these measures, we offer another approach to viewing and gauging educational success, and it starts with you. *Rethinking Multicultural Education: Teaching for Racial and Cultural Justice* (Au, 2014) is an incredible starting point for educators who view sustainability as a part of a healthy and successful school community. Sustainability means that the processes and practices of the organization can flow at a fair and just pace. The status quo may feel sustainable to those in the school building who benefit from those practices but unsustainable to those who do not. Have you ever worked with a student who disrupts the classroom lessons and whose family seems resistant to any solution-building? Those moments feel unsustainable. Those moments, to educators, are experiences that, should they continue, the student or the teacher may need to exit the system. Those moments feel like "something has got to give" and that something is often punitive measures toward the student and sometimes the teacher, administrator, or counselor. There is no harmony in these instances.

Rethinking Multicultural Education is one tool that addresses the status quo and invites educators and students to consider a healthier, inclusive, and justice-oriented way to interact with the school. This is an offering to find educational success in a way that is not measured by standardization or perfect attendance. This text, filled with chapters about bilingualism, testing, culture, history, stereotypes, and so much more, is a window into what might assist educators in building a schooling experience that affirms everyone in the building; an experience that does not chip away at the humanity of educators, students, or families. Let's take a moment to review Chapter 27, "And Then I Went to School," by Joe Suina. This chapter explores the link between a student's home environment and school community. The author describes feeling confidently situated in their home community. The traditions and relatives in his life contributed to a safe and warm experience. A stark contrast happens when he enters school for the first time. He describes unfamiliar and odd symbols and practices. This is jarring. This is unwelcoming. The reading materials were stale and irrelevant to his lived experiences many miles away. Returning home after this boarding school environment changed him as a person. From what we as educators know about Indian Boarding Schools, is that one goal of these institutions included ridding children of their home cultures. How do our schools intentionally or unintentionally engage in those same practices today?

Sustainability also means engaging with texts and questions of this nature. In districts where books are banned and public education is threatened, educators must be careful and cautious about how they engage in multicultural work long-term. This applies to educators in racially homogenous schools as well. Collaborate with your thought partners and trusted colleagues on safety plans that may further your goal of creating a more sustainably successful environment.

The Racial Literacy Development Model

Dr. Yolanda Sealey-Ruiz created a racial literacy development model that can be referenced as another empowering tool for self-reflection. Refer to Figure 4.1 and then consider engaging in critical self-reflection.

"The adoption and practice of color-blind and culture-blind research … approaches can potentially lead to the dangers of exploitation and misrepresentation of individuals and communities of color." For instance, sociologist Amanda Lewis found in a 2001 study that many

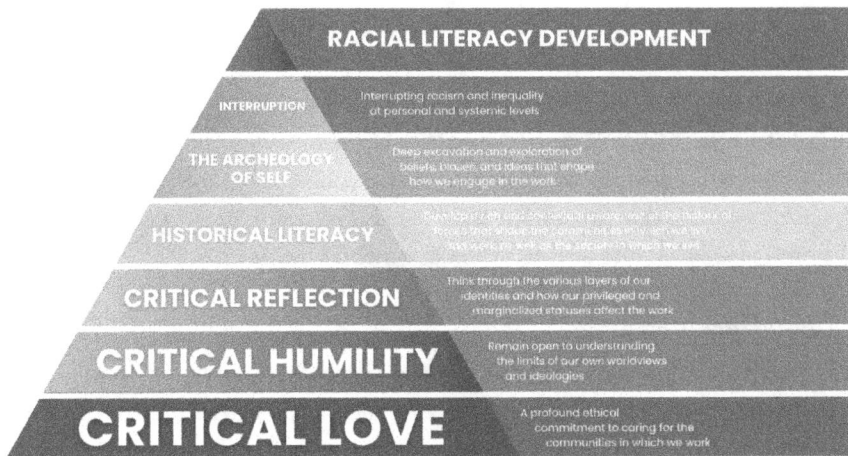

RACIAL LITERACY DEVELOPMENT

INTERRUPTION — Interrupting racism and inequality at personal and systemic levels

THE ARCHEOLOGY OF SELF — Deep excavation and exploration of beliefs, biases, and ideas that shape how we engage in the work

HISTORICAL LITERACY — Developing a deep and critical understanding of the history of forces that shape the communities in which we live and work as we use our expertise to teach we are

CRITICAL REFLECTION — Think through the various layers of our identities and how our privileged and marginalized statuses affect the work

CRITICAL HUMILITY — Remain open to understanding the limits of our own worldviews and ideologies

CRITICAL LOVE — A profound ethical commitment to caring for the communities in which we work

Figure 4.1 Sealey-Ruiz (2020). The racial literacy development model. Arch of Self. NCTE Policy Brief.

teachers and adults refused to discuss or acknowledge the ever-present social and institutional race-related matters in their mostly white school. When a student of color, Sylvie, brought up racist experiences, the teachers in the community ignored her concerns and rationalized that she was "playing the race card" (Lewis, 2001, p. 788).

The adults in this context adopted an unhelpful and unhealthy color-blind approach to their work and lives, which is a predictable response when self-exploration through an identity lens is minimal or nonexistent.

Upon first glance, what does each level mean to you as a practitioner in a school?

There is no right or wrong answer. Remember to show yourself compassion and patience as you journal or discuss your way through this model. Your understanding of these levels matters to who you are, how you have been raised, how you are treated in your place of work, and your meaning of the world around you. Appreciate your perspective and consider the flexibility that growth invites us to embrace. Together, we'll explore each level:

Critical Love

The ongoing debate about whether or not it is necessary to love your students in order to counsel and educate them effectively surfaces at the beginning of each school year, particularly on social media. Do you care about the community you serve as an educator? How do you know? How do your students and family know? What evidence would they share to demonstrate this? Do you love some students and not others? What contributes to this? Often, we show particular care toward people within our affinity groups, people we identify with because they are similar to who we are now or who we were in the past. Developing a critical love across differences is possible and requires attention and intention.

Critical Humility

How do you show honesty that reflects not being the expert in all areas, particularly your students' lived experiences and truths? Have you ever apologized to your students? What is your relationship like with apologies? Do people of authority and power ever apologize to you? For what? When? What evidence would your students share with someone that demonstrates your honesty about *not* being the expert about a particular area? Do you believe some people deserve sympathy or empathy while others don't? Who does not deserve empathy? When have you not deserved empathy? Did you receive it anyway? What did that feel like to you?

Critical Reflection

What do you know about yourself? Do you see yourself, your family, and your home community as a standard (how others should live)? Do you believe your way of life is best for everyone? Why or why not? How often do you think about this? Educators are not often given the space to sit and be mindful of our lived experience compared to our students. The school year begins, and we cruise through the last day of school, sometimes pausing for self-care or critical reflection about our lessons and practices but rarely about ourselves. Here is your invitation to take a moment and address the questions above.

Historical Literacy

Chapter 1 was devoted to contextualizing, placing a brief history of education in context for us. What we may have learned and what may have been unknown set the stage for our present-day circumstances and opportunities. Cherry-picking the histories that shape us is disingenuous and dishonest. We are shaped by all of history and we must understand all of history if we are to learn from its lessons. How much more do you want or need to know not to repeat the ills of the past? Which ills do you observe repeating today? What lessons is your social studies and history department teaching that directly relate to aiding in this self-discovery for the students in your building? What is the historical context of your school, such as the example in Chapter 1 by M Kramer, that your community continues to contend with? How does this context impact you as a person and as an educator?

Archaeology of Self

This chapter, which focuses on the deep dive into who we are, what we believe, and why and how this impacts our influence and relationships with others, particularly our students, can be summed up into what Sealey-Ruiz (2022) calls an archaeology of self. An archaeology of self allows educators to rediscover their own ideas and beliefs, especially concerning our identity. Schools should promote and encourage these opportunities as a part of how the system changes. Our students deserve attentive, caring, and intentional educators. We deserve caring and intentional school communities. How that creation happens is up to us collectively, and one of the ways we achieve the healthiest possible environment is by changing the system by changing ourselves.

Interruption

At this stage, educators have what they need to confidently and critically engage in their surroundings because they are self-aware, educated about the context and history of their role in education and schooling, and prepared to take on the difficult work of ongoing growth. In a sense, every stage of this model suggests interruption to the status quo because we refuse to accept life entirely as it is handed to us. We are playing an active role in our school as leaders and authentic individuals to contribute to a greater good, a more significant cause: the education of the next generation.

Doing Better Than the Status Quo

The status quo teaches us that objectivity is possible, but reality teaches us that objectivity is impossible. Not only is objectivity impossible, it shouldn't be a goal. Most educators have been educated and trained to understand the world through "objective facts." We learn how to structure a sentence, use tech tools to scaffold, recruit students to a small counseling group, or create an agenda for a board meeting. Most of us don't give these tasks a second thought. Reality shows us that even the mundane tasks we encounter each day contribute to a greater issue and a larger sense of perceived objectivity. When we are inflexible about what we think is objective, we are bound by traditions and practices that may not serve us well. For example, we may believe our policies and school rules are objective. People can view not wearing pajamas to school as a universal and obvious rule. It isn't universal nor obvious to some. You may have been raised in a household that viewed pajamas as inappropriate school attire. Some communities in other parts of the country or state view this policy as unenforceable and, therefore, exclude it from any handbook. While some of the rules and practices we use in our school may seem natural or common sense, they all stem from our perceptions about what is and isn't acceptable. Our perceptions are not objective. Our perceptions derive from our beliefs, values, and experiences. Is this to say all schools should make pajamas an acceptable part of the dress code? That's not for us to decide. The point is to recognize that we must make interrogating the status quo (i.e., how our institution functions as a standard) a habit, taking nothing for granted as simply "that's just how things are here." How your school functions and makes rules may not be working for certain groups of people and this can be better understood when the rule-creators are privy to their subjectivity.

Make It Work:

Unpacking this example further, we are asking you to think from multiple perspectives as a part of finding flexibility and nuance: (1) Why may pajama-wearing not be absurd to some students or families? (2) Have I assumed that everyone who attends and works at my school shares my values? (3) Can I create rules and policies at my school that acknowledge their subjectivity? If so, how? Social media is often ripe with debates about professionalism and what is appropriate vs what is inappropriate. Have you ever considered where rules come from, who creates them, and why they were created? Do the rules benefit you? Who do the rules not benefit, and why? When we think of the status quo, we don't often reconsider what stabilizes the status. What are the rules and policies in place that keep the school functioning as it does, and what do we think about all of it? Here is another invitation to start or continue thinking through what this means to you as a person and as an educator. By no means are we suggesting rules and policies shouldn't exist. Every organized society has boundaries so that it can function and people can be safe. What is being suggested is that you pause, untangle yourself from how your school functions, and consider that some of these ways may be more about compliance and efficiency for the adults than safety or health for the children. Conclusively, the status quo is about maintenance, and we may want to think twice about maintaining what doesn't work for every student.

Harm

There is joy in bringing your full self to education. There are also cautions some must still take bringing their full selves to education. Numerous present-day examples exist of educators being penalized for being who they are. Teachers, administrators, counselors, nurses, paraprofessionals, social workers, and other school staff bring identities that others learned to exclude within the school community. Being in a community with other people is not a promise of ease. Throughout the world's history, people have learned to live together. In some historical instances, people refuse to live together. This is not a suggestion to find a utopia. This is an opportunity to be honest about what it means to be in a community across differences.

There is a difference between living your authentic self and causing harm to others. We must contend with ideas that the simple existence of difference is in and of itself harmful to others. No longer can our society afford to leave our personal beliefs unattended. What do we do with the beliefs we hold for others? How do we respond to other educators and students who activate our negative associations with certain groups of people? For example, education researchers often discuss the "soft bigotry of low expectations" (Douglass-Horsford et al., 2019). Write out your answers to the following questions:

Do you ever feel compelled to set different expectations for certain groups of students who share a common identity? Where does that come from?

For some, the line blurs between being your authentic self and being someone who harms other people, whether it be through soft bigotry or refusing to share a classroom with a queer student-teacher. You may be an educator who has never experienced consequences for treating another person inhumanely. There may also be a sense of power and privilege that attaches itself to being in the majority. All of these characteristics surface when in an educator role. Participating in a school community effectively means coming to terms with what you bring into the community and committing to do no harm.

Consider what your relationship is like with forgiveness, harm, and accountability? Reflect on this!

While one educator is not the sole contributor to school system health or harm, the power of our roles gives us immeasurable influence on our school communities. Some educators use their influence for control. Some educators use their influence for positive change. Some educators don't recognize or own their influence.

What kind of educator do you want to be? What kind of educator do you want to model for your colleagues? What kind of educator do you want modeled, so that you can emulate a leader in your school?

Author and social justice facilitator adrienne maree brown (intentionally lowercase) teaches us about fractal change. Fractal change is a practice-what-you-preach type of approach that allows for small but steady change over time. This change directly reflects your values and goals and can shift systems and societies on a macro scale. Every day, a commitment is made to think and behave in alignment with stated values and goals. If possible, map this out for yourself and place the values and goals in a visible space. Determine how you will remain answerable to these short- and long-term goals. Lastly, be sure to remain answerable to the students in your community. How will you know if your change is positively impacting their lives?

When Representation Isn't Enough

For marginalized educators, counselors, and administrators, you are not exempt from discussions related to changing systems, racism, inclusion, and power. There is a complex interweaving of historical oppression and current discrimination that affords us a window into the lives of our most marginalized students. Chinese-American author and social activist

Grace Lee Boggs and Scott Kurashige (2012) explicitly described how oppressed groups internalize oppression. Her commentary points to how that internalization can lead marginalized people to marginalize others. The call to confront these characteristics is profound and a part of the self-exploration necessary for everyone.

Schools can be sites of harm and/or healing. The two are not mutually exclusive. There can be a classroom where Black girls are being uplifted while queer Latina students struggle to find community. These are the complexities of our environments. We cannot assume that just because our colleagues are of any particular marginalized group, that this means they automatically provide healing. Every educator can benefit from racial literacy development, personal healing work, and community care. The process may differ depending on a person's identities and lived experience.

Doing the work of building and rebuilding a healthy school culture with healthy adults and children requires self-work. Because racism, ableism, sexism, and other harmful -isms are in the air we breathe and the water we drink, it is not enough that we *intend* to do good. Our impact must show that we are changing the system to benefit all children. The internalized harmful messages many educators receive while being educated in schools can influence our practice. Seek guidance and support to heal those wounds and show yourself grace when needed.

Together, we can understand and shift our lives. In turn, we understand and shift the systems in which we work. Self-reflection can aid us in knowing ourselves so that we can know our students. As a community, we find our areas of strength and affirm what works for a better education.

Key Ideas:

- Educational revolutionaries of the past and present share why educators must practice self-reflection and self-awareness as an integral part of growth and learning.
- Educators must confront their past to grow as healthier educators for students and families.
- Educational systems often do not support educator self-reflection as a fundamental part of professional work. Administrators and district leaders must aid in this change.

Doing the Work

In each Doing the Work section, we will take the learning from the chapter and apply it to self-work, collaborative work, and professional learning work. To impact change, we must do the work.

Self-Work

This chapter is peppered with questions that embody self-work. Please journal your responses or discuss your beliefs with a loved one or therapist. Because most professions do not create opportunities to focus on who we are as people and professionals, this chapter should be revisited as needed throughout your career.

1. Do you identify closely with the students you serve? Their families? How so or why not?
2. How do you connect with your colleagues and students given your ability to identify or inability to identify? What steps have you already taken to strengthen these relationships?

Collaborative Work

Create affinity space at your school among the adults and children. White educators should consider focusing their affinity space on equity to address the needs of your school and better understand what whiteness is. Think through the demographics of faculty and staff, and see what may be needed. Create spaces with asserted goals. Use the tools in the resource guide to assist you. Such groups already exist in educator circles throughout the country. Seek them out and learn from them.

Create a small group book study of any of the books listed in this chapter. Be sure to collaborate by listing action items the group agrees to accomplish by the next school year based on the book's themes.

Professional Learning Work

These suggestions are stratified to promote growth within specific identities. These are healing strategies that specifically pertain to your race and racialized experiences.

People racialized as Black – Systemic change requires grappling with how systems have been oppressive to you. Focus on both healing work and anti-racism work by (1) maintaining a brave affinity space, (2) setting boundaries around helping others, (3) learning your history, and (4) building small communities that engage in the first three steps.

Black, Indigenous, and People of Color communities – Dr. Jennifer Mullan (2023) suggests a co-creation of new pathways: (1) re-educate yourself on your history and ancestry, (2) safety plan within a community of like-minded individuals who can call you in when you are being harmful or comfort you when you have been harmed, and (3) collective accountability toward action and showing up for marginalized youth.

People racialized as white – (1) School-wide book study of Gholdy Muhammed's (2020) book *Cultivating Genius*. (2) School-wide, school-year-long completion of *My Little Ikigai Journal: A Journey Into the Japanese Secret to Living a Long, Happy, Purpose-Filled Life* by Amanda Kudo (2018). (3) Invite Dr. Sealey-Ruiz and Dr. Acosta to provide professional development for your institution.

References

Au, W. (2014). *Rethinking multicultural education: Teaching for racial and cultural justice.* Rethinking Schools Publication.

Boggs, G. L., & Kurashige, S. (2012). *The next American revolution: Sustainable activism for the twenty-first century.* Univ of California Press.

Diamond, J. B., & Gomez, L. M. (2023). Disrupting white supremacy and anti-black racism in educational organizations. *Educational Researcher, 54,* 0013189X231161054.

Douglass-Horsford, S., Scott, J. T., & Anderson, G. L. (2019). *The politics of education policy in an era of inequality: Possibilities for democratic schooling.* Routledge.

hooks, b (1994). *Teaching to transgress: Education as the practice of freedom.* Routledge.

Kudo, A. (2018). *My little ikigai journal: A journey into the Japanese secret to living a long, happy, purpose-filled life.* Macmillan Science and Education.

Lewis, A. E. (2001). There is no "race" in the schoolyard: Color-blind ideology in an (almost) all-white school. *American Educational Research Journal, 38*(4), 781–811.

Muhammad, G. (2020). *Cultivating genius: An equity framework for culturally and historically responsive literacy.* Scholastic Teaching Resources.

Mullan, J. (2023). *Decolonizing therapy: Oppression, historical trauma, and politicizing your practice.* Norton.

Sealey-Ruiz, Y. (2022). An archaeology of self for our times: Another talk to teachers. *English Journal, 111*(5), 21–26.

5

STUDENTS AND YOUR SCHOOL
COMMUNITY

There may be many reasons why you have chosen a career in education. The most commonly noted among the reasons why educators enter education is to help others. We see ourselves as helpers, and through our education and training, we learn to help people through education. We enter schools with the will to do good and make the world better. How we arrive at making the world a better place differs, but what remains the same is our shared place and space. "Place and space" is often referred to in social justice circles and communities where the interactions' location matters. Have you heard of "safe spaces"? This is usually where people gather and feel safe to be themselves and connect to others who may be different from them in many ways. Schools are such places and spaces, yet we don't spend nearly enough time understanding how our differences in places and spaces make our interactions richer or even more challenging. Let's further discover how we, as educators and administrators, engage our students within our school community.

Place and Space

In Chapter 3, we reviewed some basics about how schools function, and we were provided a comprehensive overview of the systems in which we function. A better understanding of school systems allows us to gain perspective as well. Perhaps you've only worked in a public elementary

DOI: 10.4324/9781003423126-5

or private upper school. A foundational overview of schools and how they operate allows us to explore options and learn from other systems at work. Educators educate in silos, sometimes only learning from others in their department or their building. As we shift our habits and practice into more communal types of learning, we can appreciate what other systems in a school do that work for both the people inside and outside of the school.

Our place is in schools; our space can be the classroom, counseling office, or administrative suite. Within those places and spaces are the daily, often minute-by-minute opportunities to help, counsel, advise, guide, and support. Educator conversations often exchange ideas about what our places and spaces physically look like. Do we have live plants and posters of people to add warmth to our offices or classrooms? Are there pictures of your family or other students on the walls of your classroom or counseling suite? When someone walks into your space, what do they observe about the educator who works there? Place and space can evoke feelings of community, belonging, isolation, or a false sense of neutrality. The appearance of a room can signal inclusion. A teacher may place a sign in the door window about their classroom being "No Place for Hate." In some districts, this type of virtue signaling may be penalized. A school psychologist may have a picture of their same-sex marriage wedding photo on their desk. In some states, this may be welcomed. In others, it may be punishable by termination. We have seen both of these examples play out in our recent history. Some educators don't give a second thought to what their spaces mean to others who share it. While the areas within our schools can intentionally or unintentionally reflect our values and priorities, we should consider the actual experiences of students and families within the confines of our schools. So, in addition to our places and spaces showing others how our school chooses to be visually perceived, we must also consider who makes up our school community and why it impacts any kind of systemic change we collectively hope to make.

In the book *Pedagogy of the Oppressed* the author, Paulo Freire, comments extensively about dialogue. In many present-day institutions, dialogue is referred to as the action. Having conversations with students, families, and colleagues is the work to be done to impact or change the system. Educators may believe that if our conversations are courageous and we discuss what is happening in our places and spaces, we will discover solutions that can minimize, if not close, the opportunity gaps. Freire might disagree, as do many educational scholars who have witnessed pervasive nonaction facilitated by endless dialogue. Too many educators discuss without action. To Freire, the discussion and action coexist and rely on each other to carry out meaningful and observable change. We believe Freire means that dialogue is one tool that can help educators better grasp what is happening in their institutions and its impact on the greater society in order to enact change in oppressive systems. This process does not center on the educator but must include the educator. This process is not limited solely to a better understanding of one's situation and history, as you explored in Chapter 4. Dialogue to wholly understand, empathize with, and act in collaboration with your students and their communities is a significant part of the process. Dialogue that seeks to engage others is a goal. Dialogue that challenges preconceived notions inherited from ancestors and family members is a goal. Dialogue to embrace the environment your students want to learn in is a goal. Dialogue without action inhibits necessary growth and the change we charge all educators reading this book to undergo. Do not simply discuss issues at your school; actively engage in the cycle of dialogue *and* action.

Similarities and Differences

Here, let's pause and reflect on what this means:

> What is it like to be an adult in your school?
> What is it like to be a student in your school?
> Do you believe this is a shared experience everywhere in the country?
> In the world? If so, what is similar? If not, what is different?

Participate in answering these questions with a loved one to practice reflecting on the experiences within your school community. If you've never reflected on these questions, give yourself time to thoughtfully explore what shapes your responses.

Human beings share many similar characteristics. It's why we suggest books on parenting to other parents: because we believe many children are the same and will respond to various types of discipline in similar ways. We have categories for types of parents and stages of childhood development because we, on some level, believe that many human beings will share almost identical lives. This idea is also the reason behind why we teach the same subjects: because we believe many, if not most children need similar lessons. These lessons are the perceived foundation of what a person can need to know throughout their lives whether they enter work directly after compulsory schooling ends in 12th grade or whether they enroll in college or a trade. Districts and states set educational guidelines based on the premise that children need much of the same learning. What makes us as practitioners and our students similar can be maximized by our efforts to collaborate and bond, but what makes us different is the soil from which we grow into unique flowers. How we understand and relate to differences will impact how students and adults experience our schools, arguably more than our similarities. In some respects, similarness is the easier part. We can agree and have fun over pizza and Pixar movies, but wars overseas and gender expressions are where we struggle to join because of how these topics impact and polarize our families and communities. We will cover differences in a moment. For educators, maximizing our similarities can be a joining approach to building community within our schools. Many institutions already engage in these types of joining and community-building efforts, such as pizza parties, movie nights, fundraisers, and athletic events. Let's take three primary areas of school counseling for example, because every educator in every school will likely agree that these three areas serve as a primary purpose for schools to exist. This is also an opportunity for all educators to gain a better sense of what school counselors are in schools to accomplish.

Academic Similarities

Most educators can agree that all students can find joy in learning. It drives many of us to adapt our classroom lessons and develop engagement methods because we believe there are similarities among children of all developmental levels. Most people, if not all, have the desire to learn. As a society, we usually believe this. While many theories of learning exist (extrinsic and intrinsic motivation, self-determination, social cognitive, etc.), any educator will tell you that throughout each day, students in grades PreK through 12 wonder about something; even if it's not what is being taught in the classroom and particularly if what is being taught is not culturally relevant or responsive. Children question. Children wonder and ask. Joining with students about their questions is a commonality educators can use to strengthen relationships and community. Embedded within school policy and practice can be space for students and their families to contribute their perspectives and wonderings. This can be a point of entry, and often is, for school counselors. School counselors spend time with students and their families to gain a sense of how outside-of-school life influences in-school life. School counselors have perspectives about how this influence is demonstrated in the classroom or in the lunchroom. For example, a student who might be disruptive during English lessons and storytime may be sent to the school counselor for behavior when, in fact, the student finds the book topics to be unrelatable and uninteresting. Low grades can be a signal to educators that a subject is misunderstood or unlearned by the student, but it can also be an indication that a student has concerns that supersede classroom requirements. So, if most educators believe that students can enjoy learning and that most students can learn, how are all of these truths reconciled and navigated? Rely on the similarities. In her book, *The Dreamkeepers*, Dr. Gloria Ladson-Billings (1994), a former teacher and present-day educational researcher, emphasizes a familial learning environment where everyone works together to create a place and space where learning is joyous. This must involve attention to differences, which we will capture later in this chapter. This also involves four culturally relevant social relational practices that Ladson-Billings outlines as follows:

a. Educators and students must have relationships that extend beyond the classroom such as a "Good luck" and high five before a school basketball game, a chat with a guardian in the school parking lot, a kind interaction during a community festival, or an evening phone call to praise the student's in-school achievement.

b. All students in the classroom feel connected to the educators in the building. Each student is greeted in the morning by the administration. Every student gets a special handshake before entering class. Each student has an opportunity and gets a chance to pose a question throughout the school year or have their work, with permission, displayed for exemplary completion. Not one student is left out.

c.   Competitiveness is limited to fun activities and not the serious fun of learning. There cannot be space for students to feel like they are academically competing with one another. This must be a school-wide agreement. Community means every student is accustomed to learning together and sharing their wisdom with each other as common practice.

d.   Collaboration is an expectation. Social learning theory is an idea that marks observing, imitating, and reinforcement as how students learn. Educators can amplify collaboration and social learning theory when students work together, observe, and imitate each other with reinforcement and guidance from the educators who support them. Community norms in the classroom are a direct way of embracing collaboration. Students must create the rules for their space. All students should have a say in which norms are adapted for their community. Teachers and counselors should guide the dialogue that emerges from this norm creation so that students can practice being in unison.

The impact of these practices on academic achievement cannot be separated from behavior. In fact, the human condition cannot be categorized or siloed into compartments. The human condition is intertwined and inseparable. This is also our similarity.

The focus of this subsection is to highlight how we are academically similar. This may surprise you because we didn't discuss content at all. We are purposefully setting the conditions in which children achieve. This will have a bearing on all subjects.

Social-Emotional Similarities

Across cultures, many facets of our daily lives are the same. We generally experience a range of emotions. We experience emotions to varying degrees and life impacts our emotions and how we might interact with others. Our common human condition is to feel and be impacted by those around us. This doesn't change for those in schools. Can you remember a time when a student in your class or your office was in a sour mood? Did that have an impact on others? If so, how? Approaching these common experiences means we can build community with our shared experiences. Is there a community issue at school or in the larger neighborhood that upsets your students and families? What about excited and eager? Responding and preparing for these instances can be another gateway to strengthening your school's climate and culture. Shared social-emotional experiences are why many elementary and middle schools have small groups for students, and faculty have rooms to share birthday cake or sit for a shared lunch. We endure the same emotions. This isn't to suggest we all are excited about the new low-income housing development that will give hundreds of new students access to our well-resourced school, for example, but we all will have emotions related to the change. Placing effort in strengthening these ties can go a long way if we center our similarities to build rapport. When students and families can share their ways of engaging others and emoting, we are both learning from each other and being given models of community. This can often be observed at school board meetings. Sometimes, the place for highly contentious debate, what can be agreed upon is that community members want to feel heard. This is a similarity that schools must embrace. Again, in keeping with Freire's call to action, the dialogue is not the goal in and of itself. What happens after the school board meeting matters. What happens after the school-wide town hall about the new residents in the neighborhood matters. What happens after the student and guardian meeting to re-enter the school after suspension matters. What happens after receiving complaints about excluding the "Donuts with Dads" event matters. Robin DG Kelley (2022) writes about the power of art. Many educators also know this to be an often underappreciated medium for expression, not in an attempt to quell resistance to the system but as an outlet to share what may be dangerous to share in other ways. Kelley shares that spoken word, poetry, and other expressive art forms have long been a way for students and communities to communicate their pain, their joy, their struggle, and their hopes; all shared emotions. Schools must create these spaces and be open to the criticisms they will inevitably receive.

In this subsection, you may again be surprised that specific behaviors such as anxiety, disruptions, or noncompliance were not mentioned as

social-emotional issues we see in schools. The focus here is also creating or evolving the environment that is the soil for behaviors and emotions, not the resulting product. Educators must embody the difference
between addressing needs, behavioral or otherwise, and creating cultures
that reveal needs.

Future Planning Similarities

Whether we are focused on the details of the next hour or the long-
term vision of our student's careers and aspirations, futuristic thinking
can be daunting for those with anxiety and/or depression. This includes
educators, students, and families. Yet, schools are tasked to help children
prepare for their future. This is why we have Career Day in third grade
and high school counseling in 9th–12th. Taking the futuristic approach
gently and equitably leads to better student and family results. Some
educators build future planning into their routines, such as at the end of
each week, students are tasked to identify one activity or experience in
which they will attempt to engage. A student might note that they plan
to study for a physics exam or will remember to feed the dog over the
weekend. Other educators ask students to imagine or visually create the
kind of school year they want to have as a sort of vision-boarding activity.
How we approach the future within our schools can also be a bridge to
the outside community. In this subsection, in particular, it is incredibly
helpful to examine how your school might foster these connections as we
amplify our similarities:

1. Who are your families? What do they do each day? How do
    they help their communities? Can any of that be included in
    the school year? (For example, a student at Piney Ridge Middle
    School is raised by his grandmother, who owns a sizeable farm.
    One day, his grandmother brought in three baby goats for the
    elementary school to take turns feeding and petting.)
2. Are there businesses that would like to invest in your students?
    Maybe they hire interns or provide shadowing opportunities
    for high school students. Maybe they offer summer break vol-
    unteering options. How can that connection be fostered, and
    who in your school would be the liaison? Should each academic

department have one content-relevant connection in the community?

3. Who is represented? How does identity play a role in this process? Is your student body racially homogenous? Should your students have experience connecting with people from different identities? Why? How might they respond?

4. Using technology can open the world up to students across the globe. How might your school connect with communities in other countries or continents? Would you need support from the community to ensure this success? How will students help in developing such a program? Who will ensure its longevity?

The ways in which we are different also affect our school community. Often, we see in the media the ways in which difference creates tension and conflict between educators and policymakers, educators and families, students and other students, in addition to the myriad of relationships that exist within and beyond our school buildings. This is arguably one of the most difficult aspects of being a human being (a shared experience) and most educators can agree that navigating differences is one of the hardest parts of our jobs. Let's think through the various ways we can better understand what it means to encounter differences for the shared goal of systemically making our schools a welcoming and safe space for everyone who enters.

We will follow the same aspects of a school counselor's role because it encapsulates more of a whole-child perspective with considerations for the outside community.

Academic Dissimilarities

The academic or achievement gap is also and more accurately described as the opportunity gap by Dr. Gloria Ladson-Billings (1994). Dr. Ladson-Billings describes an educational debt that is owed to children, particularly children with marginalized identities. Education systems are designed to benefit certain students:

a. Students who can sit still and listen for over 30 minutes at a time.
b. Students who can complete homework alone or at home.

c.   Students who learn from listening.
d.   Students who can immediately apply their learning to application.
e.   Students who are not hungry throughout the school day.
f.   Students who prefer specific types of English, spoken and written.
g.   Students whose parent or guardian can advocate for them as needed or wanted.

What can you add to this list? What types of students have you witnessed benefit the most from your institution? Now, consider the students who do not fit this mold. Many students do not fit this mold. In these instances, we find differences that challenge educators to think beyond the status quo and develop educational programs that are more inclusive of all types of learners. This is why there is more than one type of learning institution. Our focus can extend beyond types of institutions and truly address the ways students and families coexist, but the system itself must be what is malleable.

When scholars speak about equitable practices, particularly with achievement and academic experiences, they mean practices that meet the needs of each student, no matter the differences between or among students. We don't just say, "Oh well, a student doesn't read on 9th-grade level, so we will just skip over them and pretend they don't exist." Educators have a duty to ensure we assess what students need and meet that need through the actions of the adults in the building. Part of being in a school community is building resources and creating plans to serve students based on their worldview and their experiences, not our interpretation of their experiences. This means listening, reducing bias, accessing our professional and systemic culturally relevant practices, and allowing students to lead. This also involved maintaining close bonds with families so they do not feel out of the plan. Dr. Tyrone Howard (2019) authors a book titled *All Students Must Thrive*, including steps educators must take to nurture healthy school environments and promote wellness alongside students with respect to their communities.

Reactions and responses to equitable practices can vary. By no means are these suggestions an indication that shifting your school's systemic practices or building connections with the surrounding community is an easy task. In fact, many districts and schools have seen legislative push-back to providing different students with different interventions. School leadership must prepare for the critics of equity. Addressing differences is a major challenge for people. We spend an inordinate amount of time focusing on our similarities without learning to embrace our differences. We aren't taught how to coexist with our differences beyond middle school. The necessary change falters and weakens if school leaders do not collaborate with students, families, and the surrounding community. As much as some may prefer to advance in life individually, our unity is what will help children thrive.

Socio-Emotional Dissimilarities

"Are you moving at the speed of trust?" (brown, 2017, p. 38). Trust-building may be key for the members of your school. Students don't owe you their trust simply and exclusively because you are their counselor, teacher, principal, or authority. As soon as we assume they do, we miss the opportunity to build real trust during incredibly vulnerable moments. Do your students trust that when they are feeling anxious, some adult at the school will be capable of helping them feel grounded? Do your families trust that teachers are not indoctrinating the class with political rhetoric? Are the administrators in your building unempathetic to a student who has just been disciplined for fighting? Consider how your school makes space for varied experiences and emotions. Discuss with a colleague what happens when two people within your school do not agree on the significance of an emotionally charged incident or occurrence. What happens when what upsets one person doesn't upset someone else? Does it matter which of these people is an authority?

Holding space for multiple truths was discussed in Chapter 4. When applied to cultivating systemic change within our schools, we must col-laborate with our community members. For example, at the height of virtual learning during the COVID-19 pandemic, student service depart-ments shifted their small group calendar to include grief groups. Some schools contacted local community-based organizations to gain profes-sional development and relearn skills to support students and families in grief. Some of those organizations gave the school ongoing and long-term support at no cost. Some even provided additional resources and information to families as needed. Consistent acts of empathy, such as demonstrating that the adults in the building recognize a need and want to address it with care, shape a schools' system. Modeling for children through grade 12 that care is an essential part of learning can impact the community in a multitude of ways mostly for the positive.

What happens when numbness is at the foundation of the school's culture? Educational scholars and practicing educators have several remedies, including culturally responsive practices, stronger artistic outlets, athletics programs, anti-racist and anti-oppression pedagogies, youth-participatory action research, and more, all of which should be explored until your school finds the necessary anecdotes to address differences. Restorative practices are one process school leaders rely on and should be implemented over time with care. What your community is restoring should also be cautiously interrogated.

Future Planning Dissimilarities

Equality can create access to all students and equity can ensure the students who most need access gain it. Our students come from different homes with different expectations. All of it must be respected for us to facilitate the work involved in planning futures. Our personal judgments about who should become a dentist and who should toil the soil must be interrogated with compassion so that we are allowing students to set their own course. Part of being a member of a changing system is catching your bias when it surfaces. This can be especially true when children discuss what they want to be when they grow up. How educators value certain jobs over others can be centered if educators aren't actively practicing addressing their bias. How often have you heard an educator tell students to study hard so they won't wind up working at McDonalds? How many of our students' loved ones and guardians work in the fast food industry to make ends meet? Differences in what students choose to do after high school are also an area of concern. Do the educators in your building celebrate college acceptances? Are certain institutions or pathways more praised than others? Are students and families using the college admission process as a litmus test for "specialness?" Carefully removing these harmful ideas and replacing them with more human-centered and compassionate beliefs will influence the system you are working to co-create.

School Communities Are Nuanced

Nuance is a characteristic that has its developmental place. It serves an important role in understanding children and helping children understand. For example, the statement "Children are mostly the same and also completely different" would confuse someone who lacks nuance or the ability to think complexly. This is not a judgment. Thinking in complex ways does not make one smarter or better than anyone else. Thinking using nuance can be viewed as a skill or one of many abilities. Educators who access this skill can identify when two seemingly opposing ideas or concepts can both be true. Our students can be similar and different. Our student's families can be involved and uninvolved. The sooner we grow accustomed to the reality of complexity, the sooner we can come to terms with envisioning a healthier and more realistic present and future for ourselves and our students (Moore et al., 2022). Life is simple **and** complex. We are capable of attending to both simplicity and complexity. We already do it in our daily lives. Schools need adults and students who think simplistically and with complexity, without judgment, to offer well-rounded perspectives on how the environment can be systematically organized.

In the beginning of this book, we asked you to shift or continue toward an understanding that leaves room for many truths to coexist. Flexibility is key. This involves unlearning some of what we have been trained in American society to do. Limiting students to only one category or one of two binaries can feel safer and familiar but does not serve us, and it certainly does not serve students, as evidenced by some of the outcomes we observe. Why? Because humanity is complex, and our students show us that complexity each day we are gifted to work with them.

Being Critical Without Being Critical

Critical thinking is the antithesis of mindless obedience or unintentional following or agreement. We can be critical in our approach to data as it informs our practice, but this means we question what is happening in our schools. We question origins, process, implementation, evaluation, intervention, remediation, and a litany of educational instances particularly when it seems to be or is shown by data to be negatively impacting students. Even negative impact must be critically understood. There may be instances where a family or group of people claim victimhood where oppression or systemic and historical discrimination is simply not present. Educators ought to be mindful of the distinctions between marginalized groups and groups that suffer because the two can be the same but don't have to be the same. Let's explore scenarios where multiple ways of nuanced thinking and critical thinking can be applied:

a. A 6-year-old white male kindergartener is required to share the blocks during active play and building time. He grows upset by this and no longer wants to share. After being prompted to share by his first-year teacher, he refuses. Is this child being negatively impacted by the rule of sharing in the classroom? Why or why not? If we learned that the child recently experienced an apartment eviction and could not take any of his toys, thus leaving him more attached to the play items in his class, would that shift our view? Does his cognitive ability impact how we might respond? What else would we need to know in order to assess what this child needs appropriately? How do our relationships with children of his background and identity impact our reaction?

b. In a fifth-grade middle school mathematics class, a Colombian-American boy is given a remedial math track because English is his second spoken language, and he does not test well with lengthy word problems. Is this student being negatively impacted by the math placement policy? Why or why not? Would it change our perception if we learned that his English-speaking skills are more advanced than his non-Spanish-speaking peers? How might we remedy this situation so that if we were to leave our school for the rest of the school year, this type of placement would not happen?

c. A Black nonbinary nineth grader is denied entry into an Advanced Placement Computer Science course because of C's on their eighth-grade report card? What else must you know about this situation and how might it impact your view? Does it matter which courses in which they received the Cs? Does it matter whether the Cs are a 79% or a 70%? Why or why not? What is an appropriate process to allow students to take courses they are interested in?

d. Is there a negative impact on Sioux 12th-grade students who wear traditional tribal regalia to graduation ceremonies? Why or why not? If a white student characterizes this policy as unfair and requests to wear Italian heritage regalia to graduation, how might your administration respond? Interrogate that response.

Critically addressing what surfaces or lies dormant in our school community allows educators to preemptively reduce oppressive barriers. "We can disagree and still love each other unless our disagreement is rooted in the oppression and denial of my humanity and right to exist" (Williams-Jent, 2021, n.p.). This quote is profound and often inaccurately associated with the late James Baldwin, who gave a riveting talk to teachers in 1963 about a student who craves knowledge about society, oppression, education, and hope. That talk states in its final paragraph:

America is not the world and if America is going to become a nation, she must find a way – and this child must help her to find a way to use the tremendous potential and tremendous energy which this child represents. If this country does not find a way to use that energy, it will be destroyed by that energy.

From this, we learn about the disagreements that can develop from decision-making in our schools while recognizing the power dynamics that determine who gets negatively impacted by the decisions.

Curriculum

Your state's priorities often dictate what your school highlights as learning objectives in all subjects, including but not limited to career placement and social-emotional learning, even if those priorities are to be determined by your school principal and the data collected from your students. Consider the following areas when evaluating your curriculum and note the suggested action steps at the end of this chapter to help you and your teams develop:

a. Narration – Where do your students get to tell their stories? How are they uplifted, supported and guided? Is the guidance toward you or the other educator's ideas of what is "appropriate" and acceptable? Are there voices excluded, muted, silenced, or not present? What do we do about those voices? Are local histories included in the stories told, particularly regarding social studies but across all subject areas?

b. Community time – When are the times of the day when students work together collaboratively on their own initiatives and self-directed goals?

c. Rigor – To some, rigor is a loaded term and can often be associated with gifted classes and exclusion, available to some but not all students. What does rigor and challenge mean in your school? How is it expressed by students and modeled by educators? Does everyone gain access to this style or type of experience? Why or why not?

Critical Race Theory in K-12 Schools

Parental concern over classroom content is nothing new. Educators balance tightropes honoring the wishes of families, the goals of districts, the expectations of teachers, and most importantly the needs of students. Those wishes do not always align. What remains true and consistent is that most schools want everyone to thrive, and how we collectively achieve that goal looks very different to different people in different places.

For example, Critical Race Theory stems from a legal sociopolitical ideology in response to other critical theories and legal proceedings of the 1950s and 1960s. Somewhere between then and now, communities mischaracterized a law-school level concept as a K-12 occurrence. What makes understanding this so complex is the following facts: (1) racism *is* embedded in every aspect of American life, (2) diversity of all kinds in schools *is* present, and (3) sometimes, students and educators want to better understand how racism impacts people. Because of these facts, which are also curiosities of legal scholars and educational scholars at the doctoral level, all types of education (or healthcare or housing or politics) can be studied within this theory. What does not happen in K-12 schools, at least we've never seen or heard of it happening, is teaching K-12 students the same information as law school graduate students. One idea that led to this confusion is that families and policymakers are mistaking critical race theory, which is doctoral-level learning, for culturally responsive teaching, a practice some educators use to help students draw connections between their lived experiences and what they learn in school (both ideas have the same acronym). If families think critical race theory is being taught before law or graduate school, they are mistaken and should be educated and informed about the absence of critical race theory in elementary, middle, and high schools. These conversations are easier to achieve when trust has already been established between the school and the larger community.

If families realize that culturally relevant teaching is taking place in their student's schools, they should continue to be educated and informed about what this means for their students and the school's responsibility to the greater community. Each district has a mission and vision that often includes all children's wellness. A refusal to understand the impact of culture on children is a detriment to students everywhere. Schools must maintain that educators are responsible for providing a well-rounded education that prepares youth for engaging in a global world where differences exist. Very few families seek out contentious relationships with schools, administrators, and educators, but a few vocal individuals can sometimes cause the most confusion. A compassionate educator might view this as one way a family seeks protection for their child. Our role, as educators, is to ensure protection for all students, and protection does not look the same across environments. It's up to us to work with families toward our shared goals.

Lastly, before we help you with some language, we want to note that the evolution and misuse of language and key terms to cast doubt or suspicion on social justice seekers is as old as the United States of America. Changing at the speed of this misuse is unsustainable. We must remain focused, aware, and steadfast about our daily discourse until our society removes the need to divide communities by our differences.

Responses to those who incorrectly believe Critical Race Theory learning occurs in your school:

"I appreciate your feedback. Can you tell me more about what concerns you?"

"We do not teach Critical Race Theory at the high school level. What is it about the book your student read that troubles you?"

"It sounds like you are really concerned about what your child is learning. Would you like to bring in a book you prefer to read to the class? Or we would happily feature it in our library, if available."

"I hear your concern. How do you handle differences in your home?"

These responses are not meant to be facetious. They are meant to hear families and their concerns. Their concerns feel real to them, though we may agree or disagree. By making time to understand the root of the issue, educators at all levels can better connect to how the school is meeting that need or the ways in which the school can adjust, where appropriate. Hold firm to the school or district's mission.

Responses to those who believe culturally responsive teaching occurs in your school:

"That's correct. We value every child's culture at this school."
"Because some of our students are from that country, we host a special celebration. Part of our district's mission is to be inclusive and welcoming."
"There is no one right way to be a student at this school, and we are here to make sure all our students feel at home."

Practice how you will need to respond to concerned families and community members. Grow more familiar with how to frame accurate responses while being understanding and patient. Some of our student's families have had traumatic experiences with schooling. We can honor their wishes for their child and be consistent with our goals for our school community, even if it is holding space for a misalignment.

Finally, your own beliefs and perspectives about what happens in your school will surface in your lessons, interactions, conversations, demeanor, attitudes, and relationships with students, families, and colleagues, especially when you are stressed or on autopilot. When you experience health, so too will your school community. So, take care!

Key Ideas:

- The similarities in our school community can be a joining approach to strengthening school culture.
- The differences in our school community can provide pathways to increase collaboration and empathy within our school.
- How educators engage students and their families can impact the health or dysfunction in a school environment. Learn from the experts.
- Your school and district provide a vision and mission that can help your school leaders address misinformation and contention.

Doing the Work

In each Doing the Work section, we will take the learning from the chapter and apply it to self-work, collaborative work, and professional learning work. To impact change, we must do the work.

Self-Work

1. Think of a student and the complexity of their character. How does your school meet some of their needs? How does your school miss meeting some of their other needs? Why do you believe this happens?

2. Think about a child in your life (your child, your nephew, a neighbor, a friend's child, etc.) and how you would advocate for this child. Is this advocacy different than how you'd advocate for the student in the previous question? Why or why not?

3. How has your school uplifted the families of your students?

SCHOOL
EXCELLENCE
SOLUTIONS

10 QUESTIONS FOR ENSURING EQUITY IN SCHOOL DISCIPLINE

1 **What is the expectation?**

Explicitly state what students are expected to do/not do.

2 **Why is this is the expectation?**

Note what this expectation is designed to promote. Safety? Order? Learning?

3 **Who decided that this expectation was necessary?**

The Board? School leadership? Campus leadership? Has this always been an expectation?

4 **What do you believe about this expectation?**

Do you personally believe it is fair, right, just, or oppressive? Do you believe it is necessary ?

5 **Whose values are reflected and reinforced by this expectation?**

Think about the students and families in your school. Does this expectation reflect and reinforce their values and cultural norms? Does this expectation reflect the values and norms of mainstream culture? Does this expectation reflect the values of the larger community our school serves? Does this expectation reflect the values of our district/parent organization?

6 **Whose values are erased by this expectation?**

Think about the students and families in your school. Does this expectation erase their values and cultural norms? Does this expectation erase the values and norms of mainstream culture ? Does this expectation erase the values of the larger community our school serves? Does this expectation erase the values of our district/parent organization?

7 **Who would have difficulty meeting this expectation?**

Track the ethnicity and race of students who would have difficulty meeting this expectation. What trends do you notice? Special populations? Minority groups? Genders? If the majority are from a specific student group, the problem may be with the rule, not with the students.

8 **What would happen if this expectation did not exist?**

What are the implications of removing this expectation? Implications on behavioral and discipline infractions? Implications on teacher-student relationships? Implications for student success? Implications for administrators? Implications for school culture? Think beyond the "bad" things that could happen. What **"good"** could come of removing this expectation?

9 **How can this expectation be revised to accommodate all cultures/sets of values? OR**

What shifts or expectations could be made to make this more inclusive?

10 **Should this expectation be removed because it causes cultural or racial erasure?**

Does this expectation decrease real threat to student safety or learning? What true tangible benefit does this expectation provide to students?

WWW.DRSHARLAHORTON.COM

Figure 5.1 Horton, S. (2025). Ensuring equity in school discipline. School Excellence Solutions.

Collaborative Work

As a group, consider ways to invite family into the learning throughout the school year. Create a list of ways to amplify student, family, and community voices. Collect group feedback to the question: What values do we elevate in our norms, rules, and unwritten practices? Within a team, code the responses for themes to address as leaders.

Further explore the artistic expression RDGK notes.

Book study – *All Students Must Thrive* by Tyrone C. Howard, *Teaching to Transgress* by bell hooks, and *Pedagogy of the Oppressed* by Paulo Freire. Watch webinars and videos explaining their work if the text is inaccessible. How might these educators describe your school?

Professional Work

Collaborate with the Parent-Teacher Association at your school and evaluate discipline policies and student-led organizations. Review Dr. Sharla Horton's Questions (below) throughout the school year to audit this policy and practice in your student and faculty handbooks.

Book study – *We Got This* by Cornelius Minor.

References

brown, a.m. (2017). *Emergent strategy: Shaping change, changing worlds*. AK Press.

Howard, T. C. (2019). *All students must thrive: Transforming schools to combat toxic stressors and cultivate critical wellness*. International Center for Leadership in Education, Incorporated.

Kelley, R. D. G. (2022). *Freedom dreams: The black radical imagination*. Beacon Press.

Ladson-Billings, G. (1994). *The dreamkeepers: Successful teachers of African American children*. John Wiley & Sons.

Moore, T., Shannon, G. J., & Scholz, D. (2022). Aboriginal educators at the intersection: Intimations of greater nuance in both-ways education. *Australian Journal of Indigenous Education (Online)*, *51*(2), 1–18.

Williams-Jent, R. (2021). Robert Jones Jr. cultivates community with 'Son of Baldwin,' 'The Prophets.' *Online Journal Article in Arts & Culture*. https://watermarkonline.com/2021/02/25/robert-jones-jr-cultivates-community-with-son-of-baldwin-the-prophets/

6

CHANGE AND RESISTANCE TO CHANGE

Throughout this book, we have explored a number of factors that contribute to or work against inequity in education broadly, but also in your specific workspace. You have considered the long history of race and education. You have explored how laws and policies are made and what that means for your district and school. You have identified action steps for your own school community in impacting the policies that are made within your district.

You have thought about the factors both within and outside your building that impact decision-making, equitable outcomes, and the culture and climate of your school. You've considered what changes will need to be made and what cultural wealth already exists within your space. You've thought about your students and families and their community outside of school and bringing that connection into the building. You've thought about your own thinking and how you integrate yourself into your work. You've considered your own educator heroes and changemakers. So far we've given you a lot to think about, some action items for each chapter, and a call to be different. So now what?

Hopefully, your mind has been swirling with ideas of things you want to DO, changes that you want to MAKE. But how? In this chapter, we will take a look at implementation science and consider how to move beyond just action (the fact or process of doing something) to change (the act or

DOI: 10.4324/9781003423126-6

instance of making or becoming different). Let's sit on that for a minute. How would education be different if we stopped just doing something and instead became different? What would that look like/sound like?

So What, Now What?

To help move from action to change, let's take a look at implementation science as a tool. When I moved from a school to central office in a large district (about 200 schools), I quickly realized that it's not possible to implement large-scale change without intentional planning grounded in implementation best practices. I would argue that the same is true even in one school. With staff coming and going (and I predict this will happen more and more) and initiatives continuously launching, fizzling, and relaunching – if we want sustainable change, we have to have a plan.

Educators need not become implementation science experts. I'll say the same charge that you probably want to say to your leadership – pick something and stick with it! Any implementation science-based plan is likely to be more successful than the typical "hope for the best" plan we see in schools. I get it, educators are busy. So let's make a plan that means real change instead of wasting time working on projects with no outcome change. That is the real evidence-based intervention.

The first step in the process is to choose an implementation change model. Your school or district may have processes in place to support this work. For example, the Multi-Tiered System of Support (MTSS) implementation model includes three phases to support change in the school as a whole. MTSS is more than an intervention plan. One caveat, be careful when you use education-focused models because they can easily delve into the traps of deficit mindset, quick fixes, and bias that we are actively trying to change. To help explore other options, we will use models outside of education specifically.

Once you have selected your process model, take the time to understand the purpose and function of each step and most importantly, how it connects to your goal.

Knowledge to Action

The Knowledge to Action model helps you to select what actions you want to put in place to see the change that you are seeking. Often, we jump straight from problem identification to intervention without intentional focus on what we actually need to do. Have you ever been to a School Improvement Plan meeting only to feel that all of the decisions were made before you arrived? Or attended a meeting where a problem is identified and everyone just "knows" what the next step needs to be. I used to joke that I could write the minutes for intervention meetings before everyone arrived. If we keep doing the same thing, we keep getting the same results. Sometimes that's a good thing – a student has difficulty reading, so we use evidence-based strategies we know are likely to work and the student can now read with more fluency and comprehension. If you were to go to the doctor for a broken arm, you want them to do the things that they know will heal a broken arm. But we're not talking about broken arms, we're talking about broken systems. As a whole, the education system hasn't figured out the magical mix of changes we need to make so that all of our students grow, learn, find joy in education, and graduate ready for adulthood.

In the Knowledge to Action model, the first step is building knowledge. We've talked about how to build knowledge around the voices of students, families, and the community about what they need at school. We want to pair that true understanding of the need with research into best practices. There are a number of excellent models that you can use to build a toolbelt of best practices to respond to the needs that you identify. To highlight a few – Culturally Responsive Teaching by Zaretta Hammond, Gholdy Muhammad's Five Pursuits, and Culturally Relevant Teaching by Gloria Ladson Billings. You have to have a vision of where you're going. It's important not only for the goal-setting component but also to keep your hope alive. This is not the work of one school year.

Once you have your knowledge base, you're ready to consider action – the beginning of this process will feel familiar to all who have participated in data-based problem-solving models. It's easy to fall into data-based problem-solving that is deficit-based but imagine the power of such a model when considering data that go beyond test scores and discipline referrals. In this first step between knowledge and action, we will identify the problem. We want to use fact-based terms to summarize the data that we've gathered. For example, students of color do not feel that they belong in our school. We might have numerical data, perhaps from a survey, but we want to make sure that we've added to the numbers with detailed qualitative feedback from our students, families, and community members. Think of it as painting the picture of the data. The numbers will tell you the outline, but the deeper conversation fills in the color and detail.

Once we have identified the problem, we will determine the "Know/Do Gap." I think this will be one of the most pivotal concepts of educational change. The know/do gap is the gap between what we know we should do and actually doing it. You'll often find examples of this in healthcare. In healthcare, poor-quality care is now a bigger barrier to reducing mortality than access to care (Drexler, 2020). Being an educator is a tiring job, often working in poor conditions with inadequate resources. I once didn't have adequate heat or air in my classroom for 4 years, going down into the 50s in my room in the winter and above 85 degrees in the warmer months. I've asked educators around the country about their working conditions and have received unbelievable responses. Educators are tired, many working well beyond their contract hours just to stay afloat. Students come to school every day and there's often not much time to consider best practices or to make a plan before the action. We can't think about educational change without calling out the conditions in which many of us work. When we consider the "Know/Do Gap"– be honest about what you see. Don't shy away from the work because we're tired. We'll consider capacity later in the process.

Once we have identified the Know/Do Gap, we will connect back to the research to see what will support a change in this gap. Maybe your staff knows that students of color feel that they don't belong but they don't have clear ideas on how to change that. Or they have ideas but they're not working. Revisit the research you've done on belonging, cultural responsiveness, and school climate, and identify areas that make a connection to the data that you have. Once you have selected your ideas (your knowledge), you begin to move around the implementation circle in a process that is continuous and ongoing.

The next step is to adapt that knowledge to your school environment. For our belonging example, your team could decide to use Zaretta Hammond's Trust Generators (Hammond & Jackson, 2015). You'll consider your school, its schedule, educator roles, and other context information to determine how those trust generators might look in your building. What would trust generators look like within your context? This is not a one size fits all for every school and choosing strategies that aren't relevant for your school will backfire possibly leading to even less trust than before.

Bonus points if the change you are looking to make centers on fixing the adults and not the kids. I find that when we are focused only on changing student behaviors, we have missed a central point in our data collection – the voice of students and families. Student behaviors, whether behavior as we normally consider it or academic behaviors like studying, test taking etc., are almost always related to the behavior of adults particularly when we're looking at data that reflects groups of students.

Once you have an idea of your plan, you will assess strengths and barriers to knowledge use. We often jump right to barriers so I challenge you to start with strengths. What is your building doing well? Don't just rely on your own opinion, use the data you collected from your students and families to paint the details that you need. Another strategy is to consider staff in your building that you know are doing well in the area. As you collect your data on belonging, you might have noticed a trend that one teacher or grade level seemed to be the exception to the rule. Students and families might have noted that this particular teacher made them feel so welcomed or had a great collaborative environment in their classroom. Maybe that teacher's advisory students excitedly shared what they were working on. You might notice that certain teachers have improved attendance over the school average. What are the strengths they bring – the strategies and structures they employ to make the change you want to see are already happen within the building. If we're not able to expand on the best practices of the few, we won't be able to see change in our schools.

Now that you've identified what's going well and who is already "doing" the knowledge we want to see, it's time to identify barriers. Again, I encourage you to consider the barriers related to adults and not students. Some students just don't want to learn isn't a valid response to students of color sharing that they feel they don't belong. Often these learner-centered "barriers" are biased at best and racist at worst. There are times when student-centered barriers are appropriate – for example: the students who live in x neighborhood have a bus that's often late so they miss advisory period. Knowing that our communities are segregated might mean that students of color are more likely to miss advisory period due to a late bus.

Once barriers and strengths are identified, we can select and tailor our interventions. Wait – you might be thinking. Didn't we already do that? We chose our knowledge related to belonging and connected that to Zaretta Hammond's trust generators but we didn't yet choose the actual interventions. Trust generators are a model or paradigm – they help you understand the types of things that help students (and adults) generate trust with others. Once we have that knowledge and decide it's the best tool to apply to the area of need identified, we have to make a specific plan for intervention.

For our example, the school might choose one or two specific trust generators to embed into classroom activities and the school day. They could connect teachers to students through a buddy system or build time into the schedule for students and teachers to connect on similarity of interests. The most important thing is that they are intentional and specific about what the intervention will be so that the school can monitor how it's being implemented. Monitoring the knowledge use will need to include decision-making about what the knowledge use looks like. Make sure that the intervention you choose is specific enough to be observable and measurable. This is an action that we often miss.

In our belonging example, we've seen this play out before – our data show that students don't feel that they belong. We may or may not even know that it's a particular group of students who feel that way more than others. We probably don't collect any qualitative data to find out details and nuances. We just see a number in a survey and decide something must be fixed. We know about the trust generators so we share the information at a staff meeting. Maybe there's even excitement and buy in about the idea – staff are ready to try it out! But 6 weeks, 2 months, a semester later, nobody is really doing anything differently than they were before. This is why our specific intervention plan and our monitoring plan are so important. It makes the action component realistic for the educator and it keeps the conversation going so that the change takes place.

A quick word about monitoring plans, we aren't going to see systemic change in our schools with walkthrough tools. I suppose there's a place for walkthrough tools in some areas and I can certainly see how they would help with management duties of the principal. But real change comes from connection, and I want to call that out here. When we have deep conversations about best practices for students that include specific plans of action and then accountability to one another, our change is longer lasting and more sustainable than when mandates are given and people comply only as long as the mandate is monitored.

Regardless of whether your monitoring shows that there was a change in action, take the time to evaluate the outcome. You may not be able to replicate all the steps that you took to collect data in the beginning of your quest for change but consider the key indicators and evaluate how much they have changed. If your monitoring shows that actions have not changed but your outcomes have – that's worth exploring. And of course, if your school really has changed its actions but the outcomes are the same, that's important to know too. We often stop at monitoring the action without connecting to the outcome data.

When you've evaluated the outcome you probably have one of three possibilities – you didn't get the outcome you wanted to see, you got some of the outcome you wanted to see, or you got the outcome you wanted to see. If you have the first two possibilities, you will start the cycle over. If you get the outcomes you need, that's great news! You're ready to move on to the sustainability piece – we'll explore that more in the next chapter.

COM-B

The Knowledge to Action process model is important for creating the change you want to see but it misses a major component of why change is hard – changing people's behavior. We can't have any system-wide change as a school or even an educational community without day-to-day changes by educators. For that, we will take a look at the COM-B framework. In this framework, you will consider three components that impact behavior: Capability, Opportunity, and Motivation. You can visit www.behaviorchangewheel.com to see an interactive tool for exploring in more detail.

Capability

People can be capable in two major ways: physically and psychologically. A great way to increase belonging with students might be to play with them at recess. Some teachers will have the physical capability to do this, while others might not. Physical capability could also be more nuanced: stamina is an important factor. Providing detailed feedback on every piece of work that a student turns in would be great but the teacher may not physically be able to sustain the work level needed if they have 150 students. For psychological capability, the model looks at the psychological processes needed to complete the activity. If you don't understand what's being asked of you, you won't have the capability to complete the task. I can be physically capable of teaching a quantum physics class but lack the psychological capability in the fact that I can't wrap my head around the concepts.

Make It Work:

- Be mindful of staff physical differences and allow for multiple entry points for any physical interventions.
- Check in often with staff on bandwidth. Educators are humans and have lives and needs outside of the school building. If a staff member is at their limit, you will need to remove other tasks in order to add a new one.
- Make sure that interventions are clear and staff have an opportunity (and feel safe) to ask questions and gain better understanding.
- Use modeling and practice to build skills. Allow educators to observe other educators by providing classroom coverage and time/space.
- Build a culture of learning within your staff. Honor and appreciate change and growth by prioritizing engagement and reflection.

Opportunity

Having the opportunity to participate in an action involves social opportunity and physical opportunity. In social opportunity, consider the interpersonal influences, social cues, and cultural norms that influence how we think about things. I am currently sitting on a couch at a coffee shop typing this. If I were at home, my feet would be on the couch and I would stretch out. I recognize that it would be outside of the norm for me to do so in my current setting. So even though I could physically stretch out or even nap on this couch, I don't actually feel that I have the social opportunity to do so. When we consider interpersonal influences and cultural norms, we also need to consider that these are often white-centered in our society. This usually includes individualistic, goal-oriented thinking with a side of perfectionism. Do staff and students in your building really have the opportunity to express behaviors that don't align with these ideals?

For physical opportunity, consider the opportunity provided by the environment. This includes time, resources, locations, cues, etc. If you want teachers to include restorative circles in their classroom but then give them pacing guides that keep a pace that allows for no flexibility, they don't really have the opportunity to do so. If we provide professional development opportunities during unpaid times like summer, Saturdays, and late into after-school time, teachers who must work second jobs to support their families will not have the opportunity to participate. Though we are focusing on changing adult behavior, I would be remiss not to mention that students often have barriers related to physical opportunities. A student who wants to take part in after-school tutoring but doesn't have transportation outside of the school bus doesn't have the physical opportunity to participate.

Make It Work:

- Consider the cultural norms that you see most often expressed at your school. How might that be a barrier or a strength for opportunity?
- Ruthlessly consider what resources staff need to make a change in order to implement the action you are seeking. Often I find that this has to do with time. Could teachers write out the lesson plans for an activity you want to see schoolwide? Of course, but you might see better implementation if the lesson plan is ready to go for them. Time is one of the most precious resources in a school.
- If you have staff that are not making the change in behavior, consider the invisible opportunity blocks that might be happening. Ask about the factors involved in opportunity, you might find out answers you've never considered.

Motivation

The area of motivation will be familiar to anyone who has ever tried to implement a change. I always say that I want to walk more places from my house but often choose not to because I don't have the motivation to take the extra time or the extra steps to make it happen. With motivation, consider both automatic motivation and reflective motivation. Automatic motivation happens, well, automatically. It is the process of emotional reactions, desires, impulses, drives, and reflexes. When I'm hungry, I'm automatically motivated to eat. It's not always so simple though – we can purposefully connect cause and effects that highlight automatic motivation. For example, when I make connections with students, we laugh and smile. Laughing and smiling are automatically motivating.

This steers into the area of reflective processes that include planning (intention) and evaluating (beliefs). I intend to make connections with my students, I believe that is a good thing to do. So I am motivated to increase that action. When I make that connection, I might be more automatically motivated by making connections with students. We are also motivated by different things. Being an educator is an important vocation. I truly believe that those who are educators do so because they believe in what they do. At the same time, we over-rely on this mantra of change-making to underpay and undervalue our educators. No one in a large corporation expects their employees to work when they are not being paid, to spend their own money for supplies, and to push themselves to the brink while being treated like they don't care enough. And if those companies do that, their employees leave. Sometimes motivators at work are money. If the action you want educators to take is not doing their job in a different way but instead doing more than their job or spending time outside of their workday, you should pay them for doing so.

There is a book titled *If You Don't Feed the Teachers They Eat the Students*. While the book title is in jest, the point is valid. When motivation is low, students are the most impacted. In our drill and test school environment, we often focus on mandates rather than motivations.

Make It Work:

- First and foremost, consider whether the motivation you are seeking is reasonable. In the knowledge to action process, hopefully you identified barriers to implementation, and motivation might be one of them.

- Consider if the action is one that requires extensive reflective processes for motivation. If so, build time into Professional Learning Communities (PLCs) staff meetings, and coaching cycles to make those reflective processes a part of the shared experience of staff.
- Add in areas for automatic motivation. Need teachers to stay late for a PD? At least provide food. If you don't have the budget, ask local businesses to donate. Not only does this impact motivation but it might remove some opportunity barriers as well.

Roles in the System

When considering COM-B, we need to determine which people within the system need additional support or intention with capacity, opportunity, and motivation. It won't be the same for everyone. While you can plan broadly for most people, you'll need to consider specific personalities and needs as well. For broad stroke planning in preparation consider the following:

- **Who is changing what they're doing?** Not all interventions require everyone in the school to make a change. Sometimes this leads to a feeling of unfairness or an unshared burden. That will impact motivation. Sometimes this means that the folks who would be implementing the intervention have a specific barrier that impacts opportunity. For example, one school I worked with had two out of three counselors who were on parental leave and then had a small baby at home. This impacted their ability to do nighttime and weekend events.
- **Who is the support system to bridge roles?** We are forever asking educators to make changes with little to no support. When learning a new school, implementing a new program, or simply changing how you've been doing things, it's not uncommon to need support either through coaching or even simply camaraderie. Don't wait for an intervention plan to fail before putting a support system in place. Create accountability partners, check in often, and provide folks who can help carry the load.

- **Who brings together data to support the implementation?** In education, we can't wait a long period of time to find out if something isn't working. We have to make slight changes in what we're doing in order to fine-tune interventions. I believe this is why we're often changing too soon. Sometimes it's hard to tell when you need a tweak and when you need a pivot. Make sure there are staff dedicated to looking at the data to make sure the implementation is working. Don't leave this solely on the shoulders of the implementers who are already taking on the lift of change. At the same time, the group looking at the data does need to have representation from those making the change both for the valuable input they can provide and so that the data team doesn't feel like isolated decision-makers in the change group.
- **Who are the decision-makers?** Without hierarchical structures, educators are often unsure of who the decision-makers are. While the principal is ultimately responsible, they can't make every single decision within a building. Sometimes who is allowed to make decisions has to do with political capital, relationship with the principal, and personality. This doesn't make for very effective decision-making. Making it clear from the outset can clear up how it will be decided to make changes in the process.

Collaborators

You may read this and think, but I'm not in charge of my building, I can't make these decisions. Or perhaps you are in charge but you're still not sure where to start. The first step is to find your collaborators. There will be different types of collaborators that you need. First, find a team that believes in interrupting inequitable systems. We'll call this group your belief collaborators.

These are your motivators, your like-minded colleagues. This group will keep the motivation up for you and for the group. You care deeply and that matters. If you consider your workplace and think that you have no collaborators, that's hard. It probably feels lonely and unsure. You may have to look outside of your school to find those people. It will be harder going, but it's still possible to make change.

Next, find collaborators who have skills that help move the change along. Who is organized and can help share the plan? Who is good at professional learning? This group may or may not be a part of your belief collaborators. As long as they're willing to pitch in, they are your collaborators. We'll call this group your task collaborators.

It will be important to include as much of your school community as possible. Both students and families can support the changes you are trying to make. Even in elementary school, students are powerful changemakers when we empower them to be a part of the change. Families will help carry the lift of the change. Think about your cultural wealth in your building and ask for help in ways that align with the values and strengths of your school community. We'll call this group your community collaborators. Once your school community becomes invested in the change you are trying to make, it can sustain that work by prioritizing the change over other initiatives that may or may not have positive outcomes.

Areas of Pushback

People do not like change. We can't go into a change-making scenario without being honest about how most people are going to respond. They won't like it. They'll complain. They will resist doing what is asked. That is all a natural response to change. Let's consider two areas of pushback to change: individual resistance and organizational resistance. In individual resistance, people resist change because of their own perceptions and needs. In organizational resistance, the organization's tendency is to maintain the status quo and resist change. We'll consider individual resistance first and then organizational.

Individual Resistance

Change Is Hard

At the beginning change takes more work than continuing what you have been doing. When first starting a new exercise routine, it feels like I'll never not huff and puff. It takes so much energy to get through the routine that I'm not sure how I can continue. Yeah, somewhere in my mind I know that if I continue, I'll have more energy overall, and not only will the exercise become easier but my day-to-day energy level will increase. I know that, but it doesn't make starting any easier. The same is true for a change in routine at school.

Make It Work:

- Have empathy for your colleagues who are expressing dismay or frustration with the change being asked of them.
- Take the time to explain the why behind the change, which may increase the motivation to overcome that initial negative reaction.
- Get feedback before, during, and after the change so that you can pivot if needed but also so that folks feel heard.

Bias

We're not just talking about changing a bell schedule. We're asking people to interrupt systemic inequalities. You may uncover bias in this process. For example, when implementing changes in the way that students are identified for honors or Advanced Placement courses, you may get pushback that certain students "aren't ready." When you interrogate that thinking, you may find bias in views about the type of students that are able to take honors or AP courses.

Make It Work:

- Ask a lot of questions. Why do you think that is? What do you mean by that?
- Ask for facts. If we're getting feedback that a change won't work because of feelings, we're going to keep going. If we're getting feedback that a change won't work because of data, let's talk more.
- Call it out. Especially for my white colleagues, do not be a part of white silence, call out bias when you see it.
- Call them in. While we call out bias, we need to call in our colleagues by expanding discussions to counter bias. Carefully consider who can take on that emotional labor within our group of collaborators.

Pushback on DEI

I think of this as next-level bias. Everyone has bias. We all grew up in a white-centered, able-bodied privileged society. We're seeing now a pushback on equity that expands beyond the individual and purposefully refuses the desire for change toward a more equitable society. Just the fact that the words diversity, equity, or inclusion are a part of a change you are trying to make means that not only will some refuse to participate but you may be running up against laws related to public education in your state.

Make It Work:

- Know the laws so you can be good trouble and keep your job. If Diversity Equity and Inclusion (DEI) is outlawed in your state, focus on the work and not the title.
- Connect the work to your school's improvement plan or mission statement. All schools have plans focused on student grades, attendance, and usually, discipline. Connect to those goals so that your work is connected to the work of the school.
- Lean on your collaborators. This will be important if you are in a situation where DEI work is not only not valued but also demonized.

Mistrust

I used to work for a principal who had such little trust by the staff that I joked that he could offer to put a margarita bar in the workroom and suddenly no one would like margaritas. If the staff feels unheard, unappreciated, or for whatever reason doesn't trust the school leadership or each other, change will be next to impossible.

Make It Work:

- Build the trust first. Try to mitigate harm to students as much as possible (because if the mistrust is this bad, there is harm), but fix the climate before you try to make any other changes.
- If possible, communicate the mistrust to school leadership. That might not always be safe to do so consider carefully before choosing this step.
- Before trust comes connection. Create opportunities for staff to know each other as people and that will help. When in doubt, the Zaretta Hammond trust generators work with adults as well as kids.

Fear of Failure

It's possible that you will have resistance to change because staff are afraid of failing. Maybe that teacher who doesn't want to try the new idea is really good at getting students to pass the standardized test. They've taught this way for many years, and that outcome has been highly valued in the past. As a school counselor, I have found this resistance in creating comprehensive school counseling programs. Some counselors had been used to being the "I'm here in my office and I have good relationships with the students who come to see me" style of counseling. They didn't want to make a change in being proactive and using data because the old style worked really well for them.

Make It Work:

- Provide adequate training and resources. Often we announce a change and expect it to happen without providing enough training for our staff.
- Listen to what they say, most people aren't going to come out and say "I am afraid of failing" but you can hear it in what's going on with them.
- Connect staff to one another to provide support. Everyone brings strengths and when we connect to each other, we all have things we can learn.

Organizational Resistance

Internal Power Struggles

I once worked in a school where, for the most part, we had a very positive climate. We had a truly collaborative leader who valued collective efficacy. One of the downsides of this was that there were often power struggles between grade levels or certain staff members who wanted to lead the work in different ways.

Make It Work:

- Go back to the section of this chapter where we discussed roles in the system and make sure that the answers to these questions are clear.

- Call it out when you see it. This is hard to do but can be effective.
- Connect back to the work so that it becomes about the actions and not the power as much as possible.

Lack of Training and Resources

You can have all of the capacity, opportunity, and motivation in the world but if staff doesn't have the training and resources to implement the change, it won't happen. Training doesn't just mean a one-off professional development either. In order to make a change, people have to have the opportunity to practice the new skills, get feedback from peers, and continue to improve.

Make It Work:

- Build training opportunities into the schedule.
- Keep making connections back to the change you seek throughout PLCs, parent events, and any other activities happening in the school.
- Ask about resources needed and make a plan to provide them. You may have to get creative with finding funding and time (the most precious resource in a school).

Poor Change Communication

It's pretty hard to make a change when you don't know about it. This is a classic education system move. Leadership roles out a change either too late or without enough information. People don't know what's going on. At best, they're confused. At worst, they're angry. Gossip starts and spreads negativity about the change. The sentiment is so negative that it's hard to make any headway in creating the change.

Make It Work:

- Make a communication plan early. Get feedback on that plan.
- Get buy-in through communication. Include information about:
  - What's in it for me?
  - What does it mean for me?
- Allow for two-way communication so that you can hear from staff about how things are going.

Unrealistic Timelines

Another constant in educational reform, unrealistic timelines are a great way to blow up any change you're trying to make. People feel so strongly that our educational system is inequitable that we need to change all the things right now. While this is understandable, it's not sustainable. This is a hard truth about systemic change. The flip side of this is progress over perfection. Some changes don't even start because the outcome won't be perfect.

Make It Work:

- Create a timeline. Get feedback. Probably still scale it back.
- Create check-ins on timelines and don't be afraid to adjust.
- Consider a Gantt Chart. This will help your school community see the timeline as a whole. There are many online Gantt Chart generators that can help.

Key Ideas:

- **Implementation science is a tool:** Let academia work on figuring out which implementation science model is the most effective. As an educator, pick a model to help you stay on track and stick with it.
- **Move from action to change:** The knowledge to action model focuses on the know/do gap and helps you move from what you know you should do to actually doing it.
- **Behavior change is an important part:** Systemic change is really behavior change of individuals in a systematic way. Don't overlook the importance of behavior change models like COM-B to consider capability, opportunity, and motivation.
- **If it's everyone's job, it's no one's job:** Consider the roles of individuals in the system for the change you are seeking. Make sure it's transparent and folks are clear on what that is.
- **Change is hard:** There will be pushback. Taking the time to consider where the pushback is coming from will make a big difference in your ability to respond.
- **Organizations in motion, stay in motion:** Organizations tend to continue as they are, sometimes resistance may come from the organization itself. Who knew they had their own personality?

Doing the Work

In each Doing the Work section, we will take the learning from the chapter and apply it to self-work, collaborative work, and professional learning work. To impact change, we must do the work.

Self-Work

When considering change, we often look outside of ourselves to see any barriers or resistance as something happening with other people and not ourselves. In reality, we are sometimes our own barrier or we are the ones resistant to change. In our self-work for this chapter, I want you to consider your own part in the changing paradigm.

What are three areas of change you would like to see in your school?

If you were to interrogate these changes, are there other areas of change that might be needed but you would be less enthusiastic about?

Ask two to three other people what areas of change they want to see in your school. Consider how the themes they bring up align or don't align with your own reflection.

When considering the Know/Do model, name two changes you know you need to make but haven't yet done. Is there one more you don't even want to mention?

Action:

- Take time weekly to reflect on your know/do gap over the course of one month. They can be small items or big items. Write them down.
- Pick one thing from your list to actually change over the next month. Keep track of how that goes and what results you see.
- Keep this cycle going and see where you end up after one quarter. Do you notice real change?

Collaborative + Professional Learning Work

For this chapter, we will combine the collaborative and professional learning work together. The process for considering change is the same regardless of the scope of the change needed. Use the questions as a brainstorming session with the whole faculty. The leadership team would then repeat the process using the feedback from the school to narrow the scope.

Whether your team is new to working together or has been working together for years, we tend to fall into routines that sometimes stand in the way of change. Before beginning this work with your team, consider the resistance to change section and be honest and upfront with one another about what might come up.

What data are we considering that indicates a change is needed?

How have we dug deeper into this data to determine the real stories behind the big-picture data we're looking at?

What changes do we think need to happen?

Have we considered how these changes would positively or negatively impact groups of students?

Do we need more knowledge to consider the changes needed?

If we have the knowledge, what is the know/do gap?

If we don't have the knowledge that we need to make the change, how will we research to know more?

Have we considered the behavior change components of the change needed? Do our staff have the capability, opportunity, and motivation to change? Avoid the trap of assuming it's only motivation, dig deep into this question.

What roles will we need to see this change carried out? Who will fulfill those roles?

What pushback do we anticipate? How can we respond either proactively or responsively?

Action:

- Use the questions above to guide working groups through the process of change. It may take more than one meeting to answer all the questions.
- Spend time considering the resources and tools needed to implement the change, make sure that the team works to provide what is needed.
- Keep going and don't stop, change takes time but our students need it.

References

Drexler, M. (2020). Bridging the know-do gap. *Harvard Public Health, Spring 2020.* https://www.hsph.harvard.edu/magazine/magazine_article/bridging-the-know-do-gap/

Hammond, Z., & Jackson, Y. (2015). *Culturally responsive teaching and the brain: Promoting authentic engagement and rigor among culturally and linguistically diverse students.* Corwin.

7
Continued Change

I have worked in the central office for almost 10 years. I have sat in countless data review meetings that consider student outcomes, changes that are needed, and action steps. I have studied equity, racism, and equity and racism in our schools for my entire career. I felt like I could tell you what institutional racism is. I could provide a definition and share a few key ideas in any given moment. But I've never thought about it in the way that was shared in a recent meeting that I attended by my Superintendent, Dr. Rodney Trice.

> When we know something isn't working for a group of students,
> but we keep doing it anyway, that's institutional racism.

Wow, sit with that for a minute. I haven't been able to stop thinking about that statement. It's blunt, it calls it out, and it's also so simple. We talked in the last chapter about how "we keep doing it anyway." In this chapter, we will explore what to do after the change starts. How do we sustain change so that it becomes systemic change?

Systemic change is one of those hard-to-define concepts. Often the definition includes the words system and change – a pet peeve where the word itself is a part of the definition. It sometimes lacks the breadth of change that we are trying to capture. We're not talking about a new

DOI: 10.4324/9781003423126-7

curriculum or a different software, we're talking about changing the way the school works or, dare I say, the way education works.

Systemic change requires work beyond one person or one educator. If you left your school tomorrow and a change you created would keep happening, then you have the beginnings of systemic change. One of the many goals of systemic change is to reduce harm on students, families, and communities while promoting a thriving lifestyle while in school and certainly long after.

We won't spend too much time on implementation here after our deep dive in Chapter 6, but I want to reiterate that our purpose in this change is to reduce harm and increase access to quality education so that all students can reach their postsecondary goals. We can only do that if we are thoughtful and intentional about gaining feedback from our students, families, and communities. Don't ever let that strand go.

In the implementation stage, you are considering the know/do gap and making changes. There will be many iterations. Some changes won't work the way you anticipate and further changes will need to be made. Perhaps the knowledge you thought would help doesn't or the actions that you want to see don't stick. At some point, you will make a change that is working and know, as a school community, that you'd like to see more of it.

So how do you move from the implementation stage to systemic change? Let's explore a historical example of systemic change. In 1907, Anna Jeanes pledged $1 million dollars for the betterment of basic education in rural schools. Anna Jeanes died a few months after pledging this funding but she left directions that the board be racially integrated. Directors of the Jeanes Fund included Booker T Washington, President William Taft, Andrew Carnegie, and George Peabody.

This would have been not long after *Plessy v. Ferguson (1896)* where the Supreme Court ruled for "equal but separate accommodations for the white and colored races." While this case had to do with railroad cars, it was widely applied and definitely impacted public education. In my own state of North Carolina, Black schools received $2.02 per student and white schools received $5.27 per student. They were separate, but they were not equal – even on paper.

This was the environment in which the Jeanes Fund was working. The fund would have no impact on financial allocations, school buildings, zoning, or district decision-making protocols. You, as an educator, might feel you don't have a lot of impact in these areas either. The first "Jeanes Teacher" was in Henrico County, Virginia. Virginia E Randolph was already employed by the district and was a strong leader. The Jeanes Fund paid for her salary to become the leader of the Black schools within the district. They also asked for a report to show the outcomes of her work. At the end of the school year, her results were so impressive that they printed 1,000 copies and mailed them to superintendents all over the south.

By the next school year, there were 129 Jeanes supervising teachers. These supervising teachers were de facto superintendents of the Black schools in each district, but they also worked on other needs of the community like public health, living conditions, teacher training, and "self-improvement clubs." Their informal motto was "the next needed thing." Most of these teachers were hired from within the community or may have already been employed by the district. But they almost definitely would not have been paid to take a leadership role without the Jeanes Fund.

In North Carolina, Black leaders campaigned to the state superintendent to request Jeanes teachers. By 1915, North Carolina had 36 Jeanes Supervising Teachers, the most of any state. Jeanes Teachers were required to submit annual reports of their work and their reports show many of the great pedagogy and leadership work we see continuing today. They supported schools in moving from vocational education to a "life-related" educational movement based on their belief in their community's capacity for creativity and leadership. They believed in their communities' ability to problem solve and support the community schools and to make demands of white authorities. They worked **for** their community and **with** their community.

Let's explore another story of change in our history. This is the story of Lucy Craft Laney. Laney was born in Georgia to a mother and father who had purchased their way out of slavery. In 1883, Laney started a school in the basement of her church that would one day become the Haines Institute. By 1915, the Haines Institute (named after a benefactor) had 900 students and 34 teachers. The Haines Institute was not only a place for learning but also a cultural center for the community. In 1916, a government-issued report described Haines as "The wise administration of the principal [Laney] has won for the school the confidence of both white and colored people" (McCluskey, 2017). Laney mentored and inspired a generation of Black women educators. In the book *A Forgotten Sisterhood*, McCluckey explores a group of women who all trace their educational journey back to Laney and the Haines Institute. To this day, Laney's portrait hangs in the state capital and the Lucy Craft Laney Museum promotes community outreach and education.

Without becoming experts on this history, what do we notice about these efforts? First, Jeanes Teachers were from the community where they worked. Laney also worked within her own community while collaborating with others across the country. What does the makeup of your staff look like at your school? Do people live where they work? There are myriad socioeconomic reasons why this might not happen. Where I work, it is expensive to live so the majority of teachers do not live there. Where I used to work, there was a high concentration of poverty. I can imagine that young adults who grew up there might have felt like they needed to leave the community in order to support their families. It's complicated, but one way that we can replicate this benefit is to increase the involvement of the community, families, and students in the decision-making of the school.

Another takeaway from the Jeanes story is that Jeanes teachers were expected to share what they were doing with data in annual reports. In the Haines Institute, the high standards of education were renowned. While accountability in schools can definitely take a negative turn, it's still important that we interrogate our efforts to make sure they are working. If we put strategies in place to increase enrollment in honors and Advanced Placement (AP) courses for students of color, we should check and see if there is an increase. If we have efforts to increase two-way parent communication, we should check and see if parents report an increase. Take the time to evaluate the work so that we can take the good and not continue to do the things that aren't working.

In this era of education, I often feel hopeless. We have entities that are purposefully defunding public education and actively working against the education of all students. I find it inspiring to look back at historical examples and think that if change could be made in that environment, change can be made in this environment.

We've considered how implementation science impacts our change efforts and how systemic change happens with time, consideration, and high standards. Let's take a moment to consider why we fail. While both the stories of Jeanes Teachers and the work of Lucy Craft Laney are inspiring, we know that the work for quality education for all students was not done. Let's consider strategies that will help modern educators as they strive for change.

Liberatory Design

Liberatory Design is the result of a collaboration between Tania Anaissie, David Clifford, Susie Wise, and the National Equity Project (Victor Cary and Tom Malarkey). It is grounded in the National Equity Project's Leading for Equity Framework and has three major tenets: that racism has been designed into the system and can be redesigned, that meaningful participation of those impacted by inequity is necessary for change, and that equity-driven work requires equity and complexity informed processes. For more information visit www.liberatorydesign.com.

I find the three main tenets very hopeful. If we support the tenets, we have no excuse to not get to work and start working on a redesign because if we know something doesn't work, and we do it anyway, that's institutional racism. Not only can we redesign the system, but we have an ethical obligation to do so. The second tenet speaks to what we've said throughout the book – in order to implement the changes we seek, we must have the voice and participation of our families and communities. Do not take for granted that this is happening or happening well. I was speaking with a colleague the other day who learned that at her grandchild's elementary school, parents are *not allowed in the building*. While there are limited volunteer opportunities, parents are not welcome to stop by the school or visit classrooms. I find this alarming – not only can we be almost guaranteed that parent, family, and community voice is not welcome here, but as a parent, I would wonder what they are trying to hide.

The final tenet relates to the idea that a race-based problem cannot be solved with a race-neutral response. Turns out that rising tides do not lift all ships. We cannot ignore the decades of what Gloria Ladson Billings terms "educational debt" that is owed to our students of color. In Bettina Love's *Punished for Dreaming*, she explores what paying back that educational debt might look like. While what she proposes is beyond what one individual can do in their school building, it's worth considering what microcosms of abolitionist teaching would look like.

According to Liberatory Design, why do equity efforts fail? One is that they don't go deep enough. They find an inclusion focus but don't look deeper into systemic oppression. Second, they are too linear, they don't account for the messiness of complex systems. Finally, they rely on traditional structures or teams without effective approaches. Maybe the team has a lack of trust, doesn't prioritize creative thinking, or is hasty and urgent rather than purposeful.

Consider change efforts you have been a part of before. It's easy to see where these errors happen. We look at our students and think that if we can create a more inclusive environment, we can fix what has happened. You might notice that according to school climate data, students with disabilities are more likely to report that they do not feel like their teachers care about them. Your school improvement team meets to determine a plan and decides that each student will have a "teacher buddy" who will make the time to connect with students weekly. This seems like a great idea, and the team jumps on it. When you look at the data at the end of the school year, you notice it doesn't change much. What happened? The team didn't consider that students might have been experiencing microaggressions, low expectations, and general lack of interest from their teachers at large. Having one buddy teacher wasn't going to impact their whole experience at school.

The buddy teacher solution was also too linear, it didn't include space for a more complex problem that needed a more complex solution. It relied on the team structure of the school improvement team which often meets infrequently for short periods of time. The team didn't have the time and space within its structure to hear from students, families, and teachers. Without hearing more from its constituents, the team couldn't make a complex, informed decision. We can see this pattern over and over in education because we are constantly understaffed and under-resourced. The education system is always trying to find the quick answer because we have a sense of urgency that is valid but counterproductive.

This chapter is about systemic change and how it's possible to create change even when the system itself seems insurmountable. The Liberatory Design has See-Engage-Act habits that can guide our work. We must see what is happening, engage others to make meaning of what is happening, and then act to address the challenge and learn from that action. We see all three of these habits in the stories of Jeanes and Laney.

Let's apply the See-Engage-Act habits to our world of education. The first habit is *build relational trust*. Parents often do not trust schools. In many (dare I say, most) cases, this is a mistrust founded in a deep truth. The deep truth is that often our schools don't meet the needs of all of our students and can actively do harm to some. Even in that reality, there are schools that do have a relational trust with their community. Imagine that your school had relational trust with the community of families that you serve. What would that look like and sound like? In what ways do you already have pockets of trust?

I can think of a parent who disliked everyone in the school and always had something negative to say. Her child struggled with behavior and academics. Every meeting was full of tension. Then, one year, her child had a new teacher. Mom trusted this teacher and that trust in the teacher positively impacted her relationships with other adults in the school. If you had to guess what about that teacher changed the view of the parent, I am sure that you could. The teacher made a personal connection and she dedicated time for the mom and accepted her nonjudgmentally. The teacher met the mom where she was and was open to ideas and change from the mom rather than bringing in her authority as an educator to tell the mom what to do. They built a relationship of trust that positively impacted the student. This is a story of a micro-change, but we can apply that same philosophy in our schools as a whole.

To apply that philosophy of trust building, we will exercise the second habit, *practice self-awareness*. We lean into this habit a lot in our Self-Work sections of each chapter. We can't change what we don't see within ourselves, our systems, our schools. I once had a counselor who asked me if I thought that her school counseling program was inequitable. I asked her if she saw inequities in our district system and within her school. She said yes. I then countered, if inequities are present in your district and your school, how could they not be present in your program? When we are all working for what we believe is the greater good, that can be a hard reflection but it is a necessary one. In my current role as a district administrator, I often have to stop, pull back, and consider how the decisions I make impact whole groups of students. It can be easy to complete tasks and keep working without considering that maybe the work needs to change.

To do that we have to *recognize oppression*. When we listen to those who have experienced oppression and we work to identify what structures have produced these oppressions, we can begin to make change. Connecting back to the quote at the beginning of the chapter – if we know it's not working and we do it anyway, that's oppression. We are here to serve children and yet we continuously oppress them by not giving them the opportunities for learning that they deserve.

But changing a system is so hard, in order to do so we will have to *embrace complexity*. There is no easy answer, no off-the-shelf curriculum that we can find that will magically make inequities go away. That's why Alicia and I titled our first book *Interrupting Racism*. We won't be able to change the whole system in our lifetimes, but if we keep interrupting even while it's complex and messy, then we will see changes. When we look at the work to get done, it can feel so overwhelming. I've been there myself, ready to just throw up my hands and give up because sometimes when you're in the tangle, you can't see your way out of the knots. When I feel the most overwhelmed, I find it helpful to bring in other perspectives. They may see something I've missed or bring a fresh perspective that can give me a new angle to work from. It's also helpful to slow down when you're feeling overwhelmed and give yourself time for "sense-making before decision-making" (Anaissie et al., 2023).

This connection to others helps me to *focus on human values*. One would hope that this would be one of the simplest habits to cultivate in education. When my colleagues and I are struggling with a decision, I try to bring us back to what is best for kids. If we are centering our work around children as people and human beings, we are less likely to make catastrophic mistakes. To do this well, we must stay connected to our students, families, and community.

When we are connected, we can *seek liberatory collaboration*. As educators, we are in a place of power, making decisions for our students and our schools. This can lead to complicated dynamics and unintended consequences. With liberatory collaboration, we are seeking diverse identities, roles, and skill sets in our decision-making teams. We create conditions for collective learning and action. With this comes some acceptable and accounted-for risk-taking – we are trying something different; there might be risks. We are a part of a collaborative team working together to create change.

Even the most collaborative teams can have conflict or see that their work is not impacting change like they had hoped. We are required to *work with fear and discomfort* as they are natural parts of equity work. In education, that means not giving up on an initiative because there is push back. It means not giving up because the implementation is harder than anticipated. As educators we love to walk away from a program and try a different one, often without leaving time and space to actually try to make it work.

At times the fear and discomfort may go beyond what is normal and the group will need to leave time and space to *attend to healing*. We see this more often in our schools now with an emphasis on Restorative Practices. When we check in with one another and give space for well-being, we can hold true to our habit of building relational trust.

We saw in the explanation of why initiatives fail an emphasis on ineffective power structures. One habit, *work to transform power*, means that groups can explore the power structure of the team and increase opportunities for shared power. I worked in a school where the leadership team was led and controlled by the principal. There was a team, but if we really looked at decisions being made, that team was doing what the principal determined. At a different school, the leadership team held a shared leadership role. While there were times when the principal had to make the ultimate decision, the team itself had shared power and the authority to act upon it.

There are times when I wonder why I've pursued this work. Couldn't I have picked something easier to be passionate about? Who am I to speak on behalf of these major topics? The habit *exercise creative courage* is a frequent work in progress for me. The National Equity Project has a quote "Oppression creates fear of change" (Anaissie et al., 2023). How powerful is that? When we are scared, we aren't creative. It's going to take a lot of creativity to change a whole system of inequity. When we have creative courage, we're empowered to think and act creatively. We encourage one another on the team to think of new ideas and to do something differently.

We can think of new ideas because we *take action to learn*. As educators, we can't wait for the answer to come on how to increase equitable educational opportunities for all. We can use our own work with students as a way to research what changes will be effective. This practitioner research means that we, as professional educators, are always collecting data, staying curious, and determining what is working and not working for students. It's intentional and aims to advance our own practice.

Finally, when we find things that work we *share, don't sell*. We aren't out there evangelizing the work that we're doing but we do invite others into our work as collaborators. When we share in this way, we also increase the possibility of questions and feedback that can actually advance our work. This makes me think about really well done Professional Learning Community (PLC). In this climate, educators share what they've tried in response to some sort of problem. The PLC then collaborates with that person to create new solutions for new outcomes. Those that listen might learn new ideas from their colleagues who share but the sharing colleagues will also benefit from the questions and responses given.

These habits are just that, habits that have to be built and practiced. Habits don't always come naturally and there are too many here to always keep in front of mind. Read through this section again and consider which habits are strengths for you and which are areas you would like to practice. Take the time to notice where you are already practicing your strong habits and situations where you need to add practice habits. Don't leave out the good parts, they are necessary to keep you going.

One way to build habits is to incorporate them into your routine. For example, I work with school counselors who are constantly on the go. They often find it hard to collect data on their work. I always suggest to them that they incorporate the data into what they're doing. If you are working with students on goal setting, use their self-rating scores as one data component and help students to track their progress to their goal.

Teaching students about progressing toward their goals is the work but the data come out of it naturally.

In the book *Street Data* (2021), authors Safir and Dugan talk about the pedagogy of voice. In pedagogy of voice, we allow students to have a voice within the actual work they are doing. It "shifts the locus of learning and power to the student" (p. 107). Some of the strategies they share for this are particular to learning assignments and are not what we are talking about here so I will highlight just a few. In "simple rule 1," they highlight a scene from the play *Hamilton* where Aaron Burr suggests *talk less, smile more*. What a great rule for living! When we talk less, we allow others more space to share their thoughts. When we smile more, we give nonverbal communication that it is a safe place to share your experiences.

The second simple rule is *questions over answers,* creating a culture of inquiry not just in classrooms but in professional learning spaces as well. We see this in our See-Engage-Act habits from Liberatory Design. We can't expect our educators to solve complex problems when they are scared to take a chance. Ask a lot of questions of each other as colleagues and from leader to staff. Interrogate the status quo. Once you've done that, it's time to *ritualize reflection and revision*. Reflection is an extension of questioning. Reflecting is questioning after we have acted. It's just as important but much less often implemented, especially in fast-paced environments like education.

I'm considering that right now you might be asking yourself, I chose this book because I wanted to implement change but I'm waiting for them to tell me what to do. Equity work is challenging and complex. Not only can I not tell you what's happening in your school, I also can't tell you what habits and strategies you need to try for your specific set of strengths and challenges. There is no linear solution to this complex, hard problem of systemic inequities. It takes a mindset shift and change. You won't ever finish, but you can evaluate how much progress you are making.

Evaluation Frameworks

Similar to implementation frameworks or theories, there are a number of evaluation frameworks that we can pull from. We'll share a few here but the same thing holds – pick one and stick with it. We are not implementation scientists who are looking for the absolute best evaluation plan. We simply want to know if what we are doing is working and to gain an understanding of why that is.

RE-AIM Framework

The RE-AIM framework is an acronym for:

- **Reach**: How much a change or intervention reaches the targeted population. If our intervention happens after school but most of our target population has to ride the bus, we'll likely have low reach.
- **Effectiveness**: The impact on relevant outcomes. Whether or not we reached our goal. If we had a goal to increase school climate scores and we do increase scores, we've shown effectiveness (or ineffectiveness). We often only look at this type of data.
- **Adoption**: The willingness of individuals to implement the intervention. For example, as a central office administrator, I could choose a program that is excellent but if none of the schools I work with actually use it, we have low adoption. Here we'll look at buy-in and readiness for change.
- **Implementation**: The fidelity of implementation with quality and consistency. We talk about this a lot in education.
- **Maintenance**: How long we can sustain the intervention. Will it still be effective and is it a routine practice?

We'll explore an example of a teacher who is working to implement affinity groups in her school. Looking at the RE-AIM framework, she first has to consider the reach of her intervention. Usually, in a school, we are able to have pretty good reach because we are in charge of how students spend their day. However, if your affinity group is during an intervention time where students are required to receive special ed services, that may impact your reach.

The next step is evaluating the effectiveness – what outcomes do expect from the affinity group? One outcome might be an improvement in self-reported belonging, another outcome might be improved grades. Go into your evaluation plan knowing what outcomes you'd like to see.

Once you have chosen your outcomes, determine how you will assess effectiveness. Remember that in a school, you aren't running a research study! Don't make it too complicated but do make sure that you are looking at effectiveness.

In this example, the teacher is implementing one affinity group. So adoption is not high on her list of things to evaluate. However, if the next year, she wanted to spread the idea of the affinity group to other schools in her district, she could look at the number of schools that implemented it and how many students participated.

Implementation is something we talk a lot about in education but we typically call it "fidelity of implementation." If the teacher is using a curriculum for her affinity group, we would want to see that the curriculum is being taught as it is written. If she's not implementing a curriculum, implementation might look like how often the group actually meets and for how long.

Maintenance is how much a program becomes a part of the organization and continues on even with staff or schedule changes. The teacher won't be able to see that right away but as she moves forward, she will want to consider strategies that will increase maintenance. This includes creating resources so that the facilitator is not creating all of the materials for the group each year or scheduling a time in the day for programs like these either in Flex period or advisory.

Focusing Direction

Having an evaluation plan will keep you on track to making the changes you seek. Once we are doing that, we can make the invisible visible. In teaching and education, there can be a sentiment that "good" teachers just have this *je ne sais quoi* – an undefinable talent for being a teacher, or school counselor, or administrator. This is a dangerous philosophy. If that is the case, then "bad" teachers have no hope of changing their practices. We just have to sit and wait for the mythical great teacher to come along. When we create a plan, evaluate the plan, and then make that plan sustainable within our building, we are breaking down this philosophy and creating change.

Think of an educator that you admire. Maybe it's a teacher that you had, a school counselor that you worked with, or a principal that led your school. When you think about them, I can almost guarantee that they had the same characteristic – they made you feel safe. They helped you to push your own limits in a way that felt exciting and led you to grow.

Zaretta Hammond calls the type of educator that I want to be as a warm demander. The warm demander is kind and caring, they care about the student (whether that student is an adult or a child). They also demand their best and never let up with their expectations for their students. In her book *Culturally Responsive Teaching and the Brain* (Hammond & Jackson, 2015), Hammond gives specific actions that educators can take to create a warm demander spirit in their classroom or school.

Street Data explores how one can create a safe classroom community through six aspects of social justice pedagogy. Their first strategy is that of warm demander and then treating students as intellectuals. We can do that by building an inquiry-based learning environment. At one school where I worked, we were an International Baccalaureate elementary school. This was actually my first job so I didn't understand at the time how unique it was. We had units of inquiry where we embedded our state standards into inquiry-based learning opportunities for all students K-5. Kids learned not only content but how to be curious and to stretch themselves.

This school served predominantly marginalized groups and it was important that we started with knowledge of our students. They typically had not traveled very far from where they lived, many students had limited opportunities to visit museums or libraries, and more than a few of my students had little furniture or comfort items in their houses. It was important for us to include prior knowledge and student voice and choice in learning so that students felt that they were a part of the experience and not that they had missed out. A very simple example is my introductory lesson where we made a classroom quilt that represented each student. I quickly learned that a lot of my students didn't know what a quilt was so I began to bring a picture of a quilt with me. Once they saw the quilt, many did have experiences with a quilt in their family, maybe with baby clothes or that belonged to their grandmother. I gave them time to share their stories and to hear what mattered to them. They got to be their true self in the discussion without needing a specific set of background knowledge to access our learning.

The next aspect is the safe classroom community – though I've been using this term in general, for this aspect, they are looking at how we protect our students – with clear expectations of learning behaviors, awareness of the mood of the classroom, and intervention when needed. The goal is to create both an emotionally and physically safe space so that the teacher can be a coach. The coach doesn't compete in the race but supports their players in doing their best. The students do the work, not the teacher. The educator is there to help students understand how they learn, academic skills, and to create a culture of practice. In our house, we have a saying "In order to be good at something, you have to be bad at something." Learners aren't able to be bad at something if they feel unsafe.

Finally, the social justice curriculum is crucial to the social justice pedagogy. We must teach about the world in a way that helps students see its complexity and interrogate the norm they see in front of them. By building problem-solving skills and exposing all students to social justice curriculum, we can help students grow into change agents that impact the world around them. In *Interrupting Racism* (2018), Alicia and I explore the use of Learning for Justice's Social Justice Standards and how to incorporate them into lessons. One of my favorites is helping students to research young changemakers who have been leaders in environmental justice, racial justice, and gender equality. Students can learn and explore children just like them who have made a difference and consider what they might learn and apply in their own lives.

How do we take these concepts and apply them to focusing direction? In order to do that, we need to also have safe learning communities for the adults in our building. Educators are always rushing and moving as fast as they can to meet the needs they see in front of them. I think this also means that we have a very low tolerance for slowing down and learning. I've always believed that instead of having summers off, we should move schools to a year-long schedule with breaks between each quarter. Some schools in my area do this as a magnet calendar that parents can choose. However, instead of having teachers unpaid and not working during these breaks, we should extend teacher's employment and use the time between quarters for intentional planning around student needs.

Likely you won't be able to change your school's calendar or salary structure. How can we take that idea and build time for educators to slow down and change the course of their instruction based on what students need. Let's look back at Liberatory Design that we explored earlier in the chapter. Which habits would build direction and focus for the adult educators who are also learning and developing their craft?

I'd like to highlight *seek liberatory collaboration* as a habit that can build our intentional work with students. When we are truly collaborating and taking risks, we can support one another in expanding our practices to do differently. We can explore the habits that will help each of us to design a system that is different than the one that we are currently a part of. Because if we do the same thing when we know it doesn't work, that's institutional racism.

Key Ideas:

- Systems change takes intention and time. We can learn from our changemakers of history to impact change now.
- Liberatory design is a framework that helps us consider designing a more equitable education system by building key habits for change.
- When we implement change, we need to evaluate our progress and adjust our actions.
- Focusing direction through social justice pedagogy (Safir, 2021) keeps the work going over time.

Doing the Work

In each Do the Work section, we will take the learning from the chapter and apply it to self-work, collaborative work, and professional learning work. To impact change, we must do the work.

Self-Work

The first part of change is doing something differently. In the last chapter, we explored how to intentionally choose the different you want to do and to implement the change in a way that will work. In this chapter, we've explored ways to move the implementation into systemic change that continues regardless of the individual. You might have been surprised how much we focused on individual habits and actions that you can build. After all, aren't we saying that systemic change is beyond the individual? Yes, that is the case, *and* change won't become embedded in all that we do if we don't build the habits to sustain it.

Consider the habits of liberatory design, which do you think are your strengths?

How can you build upon those strengths to amplify their impact on your role within your school?

Consider the habits of liberatory design, which do you think you could improve?

What are three ways that you can build the habit you seek?

1.

2.

3.

Consider your school community, including educators, parents, students, and families. How do you see examples of "Oppression creates fear of change"?

Consider your school community, including educators, parents, students, and families. How do you see safe learning environments for educators and students?

Action:

- Research an educational changemaker from your community or your state. What practices of systemic change can you identify in their story?
- Use a habit tracker to notice when you are implementing the habits of liberatory design.

- Select and choose a part of the RE-AIM evaluation framework to consider the effectiveness of a change you are making in your work.

Collaborative Work

To build safe learning communities for our staff, we can use our team time with intention and purpose. PLC in many schools has come to stand for any meeting with your colleagues and often looks more like planning than a PLC. Certainly, the framework of PLC has a structure and format created by DuFour and others; for our purposes, we will consider the broad meaning of the term to indicate a time for educators to collaboratively explore student learning with intention.

The first step might be to consider if your PLC is actually collaboratively working on student learning. Take the time to look at your agendas and see if you allow time for reflection and consideration. After that, pay attention whether your actual time spent aligns with the agenda. Be careful about time sucks like routine planning and the business factor of school life. Create a space for really collaborating.

I work as the director of school counseling in central office. I am going to create time in my district counseling meetings to reflect and consider, allowing the educators (in this case, school counselors) the time and space to be vulnerable and share areas where they need help from their colleagues. The school counselors come from different schools and may bring a completely different perspective. I am going to preselect a counselor by reaching out ahead of time and seeking a volunteer. I never want anyone to be surprised into a moment where they may feel vulnerable. The counselor will bring data to the group, it can be broad like schoolwide data or very specific like qualitative feedback from students or teachers. The counselor will present their data and the issue that they are seeking feedback and support. I want to create an environment where folks will feel comfortable admitting things they've tried that didn't work or times where they don't even know what to try. During this time, we can intentionally build in the habits of liberatory design. I might even share one habit each meeting and ask that we focus on that habit throughout the discussion.

Considering your PLC time, how much time do you spend actually collaborating?

How can you build systems and structures for your time together that will allow for a safe learning environment for you as educators together?

What structures can you put in place that will build a routine for sharing sticking points and learning opportunities for you as educators?

Do you think that your PLC is a safe environment for all? Consider that not all people have the same environment and that some of us have privileges that we bring into the conversation with us.

Action:

- After reflecting on your systems and structures for collaborating, make a plan as a team that you will implement for your next four meetings. In the fifth meeting, reflect on what strengths and areas of growth you see in your plan.
- Incorporate the habits of liberatory design into your work in at least two ways, identify them here:
  -
  -
- Once you have identified strategies that work, share with your school leadership and others who can learn from the experience of your PLC. Bonus for making a presentation to your colleagues where they can experience a safe learning environment themselves.

Professional Learning Work

Divide up the habits of liberatory design and have each team (grade level, content, etc.) teach the habits over the course of a semester or year. Depending on how often your staff meets, you will have a week, a month, or some amount of time between learning opportunities. During this time, the school body can work on the habits they've learned and share how it's going. In order to do this, your school will have to have a spirit of shared learning and vulnerability. If we only enter work spaces as an expert, we lose the opportunity to grow.

Action:

- Divide the liberatory design habits between teams within your school.
- Set aside time in each staff meeting or professional learning session for each team to share their habits.
- Build in time between learning sessions for teams and individuals to practice habits and reflect on their practice.

References

Anaissie, T., Clifford, D., & Wise, S. (2023, August). *Liberatory design deck*. National Equity Project. https://static1.squarespace.com/static/60380011d63f16013f7cc4c2/t/64e7eec1af73ab61a813bd72/1692921543446/Liberatory+Design+Deck.pdf

Atkins, R., & Oglesby, A. (2018). *Interrupting racism: Equity and social justice in school counseling* (1st ed.). Routledge. https://doi.org/10.4324/9781351258920

Hammond, Z., & Jackson, Y. (2015). *Culturally responsive teaching and the brain: Promoting authentic engagement and rigor among culturally and linguistically diverse students*. Corwin.

McCluskey, A. T. (2017). *A forgotten sisterhood: Pioneering black women educators and activists in the Jim Crow South* (First paperback edition). Rowman & Littlefield.

Safir, S. (with Dugan, J.). (2021). *Street data: A next-generation model for equity, pedagogy, and school transformation* (1st ed.). SAGE Publications.

8

MAINTAINING PROGRESS

DISMANTLING THE FOUNDATION TO BUILD ANEW

The answer to cold is heat, the answer to hunger is food. But there is no simple monolithic solution to racism, to sexism, to homophobia. There is only the conscious focusing within each of my days to move against them, wherever I come up against these particular manifestations of the same disease.

(Lorde, 1984, p. 136)

For those who work in schools and enact change regularly, the task of rebuilding a system may not seem daunting. Many have engaged with training and graduate education that prepares you for evolving systems for the better. The challenge is to maintain good progress. What does good progress mean?

Undoing centuries-old inequities and inequalities in education is no overnight accomplishment. It will take many centuries to remove the patterns, institutional practices, and personal beliefs that wreak havoc on marginalized communities. The dysfunction of a society that maintains inequity and inequality negatively impacts everyone, directly and indirectly. The cost of keeping our systems as they are has seen staggering effects that permeate every facet of our daily lives, from maintained poverty, mental illness, domestic violence, climate crises, unstable labor forces providing meaningful and fulfilling work, and so many other

DOI: 10.4324/9781003423126-8

societal ills. Despite many negative outcomes, change and reform have been a constant. We inch closer and closer to the type of world we want to live in but remain quite far from self-actualization and an environmentally healthy planet. So, how do we continue to make good progress toward unity and humanity, given our long history of division and inhumane treatment of others? We remain relentless.

Schools are organizations. According to racialized organization theory, people within schools may be racist, anti-racist, bigoted, equitable, show prejudice or favoritism, or be fair, but as a structure, the organization or institution can possess racist and classist characteristics even when the people within the building are not racist, or bigoted (Ray, 2019). An individual teacher may give special privileges to the white students in class while disproportionately sending Black students to the main office for behavior issues like calling her out for her favoritism. When a school allows this teacher's behavior to continue, the structure or institution is enabling a racist routine. Both the teacher and the institution matter. Both work together to maintain inequitable systems. Both must be addressed if progress toward more humane practices is to be assured. Some refer to this process as institutional racism, when despite an individual person's actions, there are features about an institution or organization that allow racism and other -isms to flourish. This routine becomes an expectation. It is justified. It is accepted by some, if not all, within the school. It occurs over time, and it is embedded in school practice. It may even spread to other types of anti-educational and discriminatory behavior. This is not only an individual teacher problem, a one-classroom problem, and a principal problem, but a school-wide organizational problem that reflects a more significant societal problem. For this next section, we will explore ways to identify progress and work to minimize the replication of a harmful system.

Define Community

Where is your community? Who is included? What happens within your school community? What are the words to describe it? Is there a community that helps you thrive and supports your efforts to bring about restorative change within your school community?

Through the practice of education and community service of all types, we have learned some universal truths about community. In his creative explanation guiding educators to foster community and "superhero"-like characteristics, in *We Got This: Equity, Access, and the Quest to Be Who Our Students Need Us to Be*, Cornelius Minor (2019) provides effective strategies to do one of the most simple yet challenging tasks to promote healthy community change: listening. Students want to be heard. Families want to be heard. People resist dehumanization in all forms; they always have and always will. Listening to build trust is vital, especially when there is accountability. Listening builds community and allows educators and students to pause and connect with someone within their community. Training faculty, staff, and administrators to listen compassionately and effectively is an important and ongoing duty. Students will model what they can see, and the adults in the building will be more equipped to demonstrate the school's values.

Additionally, what do we know about schools? We know several facts about schools and the people who exist within them during given hours of the day. We know that school buildings are physical structures that deteriorate over time due to weather, wear and tear. We know that school buildings house classrooms and offices with walls and maybe windows. There may be art created by children in the hallways of your school building or corkboards for announcements. The main office often has a large window, but this can often be where your administrators keep their files, records, and technology. A cafeteria may be where children eat lunch in the middle of the day. We take this knowledge for granted because we are inside and outside our buildings or structures daily. We forget that we are sheltered in the same space together, often for at least 7 hours a day, 5 days a week. That is an enormous amount of time together or not enough, depending on who you ask. During this time in the school day, we know that students encounter many adults tasked to teach them and help them accomplish their goals. Sometimes, these adults have to help students accomplish goals the students did not create. What are the opportunities within this knowledge? What can we learn from the truths of our everyday experience if we pause to reflect? What might we want to see change or remain the same in the 5 days for 7 hours that we are together? Are we making the best use of our time together? Are we designating specific times throughout the week to intentionally listen to each other? When we think of the physical spaces we spend 7 hours each day in, does it evoke a sense of learning, doing, being, or exploring? These moments of pause and reflection on just a fraction of what we know is true about our surroundings and daily interactions may offer us a window into other possibilities. What may be another possibility if you were to sit and design a school day with your students and their families? Have you ever spent 5 minutes drawing a diagram or listing words that remind you of joyful learning, heart-felt listening, and unconditional belonging? Do you even know what that experience is like to conjure an image of it? In her book *Being the Change: Lessons and Strategies to Teach Social Comprehension*, author and literary coach Sarah K. Ahmed (2018) highlights ways educators and students can practice beyond old ways of thinking. Ahmed notes how identity and background play a large role in how we think about the world, our communities, and our students. Educators must think just as deeply about topics to habituate introspection that shapes our behavior. Identifying additional information we may need or marginalized groups we may be excluding is a part of building our awareness for the benefit of the community. While Ahmed's brilliantly organized book is designed primarily for educators to use with students, we urge educators to engage in the activities she lists as a part of ongoing professional development among colleagues.

To continue with this theme of defining community as we seek to promote progress in our schools, we can better articulate the relationships between the numerous human beings charged with the education of the next generations; no small task. Who are those people? Do they represent similar or different backgrounds than the students in the school? Do they, themselves, love learning? How is that demonstrated? What kind of students were they? This may seem like irrelevant information or details that don't need to impact the educational experience in your school, but as Chapter 4 tells us, every human in the building, including the adults, brings to the environment who they are, what they believe, what they've experienced in life, and so much more. The interconnect-edness of this ecosystem's pieces determines the ebb and flow of your school climate, school culture, classroom environment, and so on. Just as a teacher can notice the shift in classroom behavior when one or two particular students are absent or present, all the pieces of your school's puzzle fit together and produce what you experience there every day. Based on the lessons we learn from the living world, we can introduce ideas and processes to positively influence the experiences of everyone in your school, including you. This is not to suggest a utopian or unrealistic imaginary new school. We honor the complex ways in which schools function at the mercy and whim of federal and state guidelines and policies. We acknowledge the funding on which many school districts are operating. We understand the restrictions because we have lived and worked within similar circumstances. It is precisely because of these conditions that we emphatically urge educators of all types to imagine a different way to educate within their communities while learning from both within and outside of their communities. A different way does not have to completely deviate from what you've come to hold dear, but it does differ from how marginalized children, in particular, have not benefited from the status quo of education in America. We must be different and continue to be different until schools are just places for all children. There are examples all around us that show another, better way is possible. Better schooling has been realized in many iterations throughout our past and even during our present. The answers are evident in what students show us about ourselves. Where we need to continue to shift is evident in our outcomes if we believe that all children are capable of greatness.

Thankfully for us, as educators, administrators, school counselors, teachers, and support staff, we do not have to figure out all the solutions ourselves. Additionally, school districts across the country are plagued with notions that they operate in silos as if the world is not constantly gifting us answers to the questions that keep us up at night or the questions that seem to cost billions of dollars to address. In community, we have all we need. We have approaches, strategies, perspectives, techniques, and programs. We hope to remind readers of the opportunities that naturally exist within our grasp. There are innumerable ways we as practitioners can imagine and reimagine our school communities with students and their families if we are so brave. We simply must look within and outside.

Community Care and Mutual Aid

As we plan to renew the sense of community in our schools, moving away from rigid and inequitable ways of schooling, there are ways to rely on what is already known: the factors that contribute to healthy groups of people. Community care is more than large groups of people caring for one another. Community care involves intention and action. Community care also involves conflict resolution and centering peace. Human beings in grades prekindergarten through college will always, and have always, experienced disagreements. This is a fact of life that will never change, and we can learn together and grow together through our differences, in celebration of our differences, and despite our differences.

Consider your community. This involves your school, the neighborhoods that surround your school building, and the neighborhoods where your students and educators come from. Imagine their strengths, the people who live and work there, and the organizations that provide various types of support to those in the region. Start a list. School social workers are often the resource experts. Be sure your list is categorized by need, and this list needs to be updated yearly to ensure proper means of communication such as email, phone number, and contact names. When schools are in the habit of being siloed, operating as their own entity and seeking to provide every student's needs, students will inevitably falter. No one organization or institution can be designed to meet *all* the needs of everyone. This is an impossible expectation. School administration, district leaders, and communities often expect schools to meet every need when that expectation is unattainable. This is why we have a community. This is why community is essential to progress. This is why other people exist with differing skills and talents to draw on. Only together can we begin to design and maintain an equitable system.

Individualism Delays Progress

Individualism is the lived practice that human beings are mostly self-sufficient. In American society, in particular, people are often taught that if we work hard in school and get good grades, we can pursue our goals as adults, all through our own doing. What is left out of that logic is that numerous factors contribute to how we live as adults. Ignoring these factors is excluding the truth from our lived experiences. Let's participate in a self-reflection exercise:

What did you do today? It's a simple question, but try to organize your day by hour on paper or in an electronic document. Start at 8 am and log your daily tasks through the time you go to bed. Be sure to note your achievements and accomplishments throughout the day, even if it was simply checking off one or two boxes on your "to-do" list.

Once you've spent several minutes reflecting on your day, note all of the tools, foods, services, and items you used through this day that you did not create yourself. For example, I woke up to an alarm that I did not create myself this morning. Someone or a group of people created my mobile device that I use to set my morning alarm. That is one example of how someone or a group of people I do not know helped me as soon as I woke up. It took only one minute into my day for me to rely on others. Let's say you woke up naturally, without an alarm. Did you make the bed you slept in? Did you grind the beans you used for your morning cup of coffee? Did you build your home? Did you engineer the water supply to your home? By now, you may see the purpose of this exercise, which is also a strategy to use with students who want to strengthen their knowledge of community. Throughout each day, we rely on others to achieve our goals. No human being can do anything in total and complete isolation. Though we may choose to ignore or devalue the impact of others in our lives, it doesn't change how we need each other to live.

Gratitude

The next step beyond recognizing how people are intertwined and connected as we shift away from individualism is showing appreciation for the various contributors to our daily success. Gratitude is often expressed at significant life events such as graduation and weddings, but incorporating gracious practice in our school culture can increase shifts away from individualism. Here are five key ways you can help embed gratitude as a foundational theme in maintaining progress in your school:

1. Lists
2. Contemplation
3. Behaviors
4. Evaluating gratitude

Researcher Malissa Phung (2015) states that "narratives of success and gratitude are integral to the intertwined processes of survival and subject formation for those who have experienced intense struggle, loss, and trauma: they constitute necessary life-writing tools for regenerating… self-existence, livelihood, being, and identity" (pp. 18, 23–24). The daily incorporation of acts of gratitude can be a deeply reflective practice that joins members of your school community as they engage in ongoing dismantling, a difficult and often cumbersome reality. Teachers and counselors can invite students to create lists, share "thank you" cards, demonstrate their gratitude through actions, and reflect on how they show gratitude throughout the school year. The adults of the building must engage in the same practices for this to be meaningful.

Visual Progress

If you are able to see, you can view the physical characteristics of your school building. Oftentimes, this is an opportunity to expand educator creativity in a visual sense. Some schools have murals on the hallway walls. Some schools have special designs on the floor to show where little feet, or big ones too, walk in line or small groups. Some teachers change their bulletin boards to match the season outdoors. Many educators and librarians display books, painting a colorful array of children of all skin colors at the library or classroom entrance. These are quick ways to surround yourself and your students with an appreciation for difference. We shared several activities based on social justice standards in our previous book, *Interrupting Racism: Equity & Social Justice for School Counselors* (2018).

Building on those suggestions here, we offer multitiered visual and spatial cultural competency: (1) school-wide level experiences such as murals in hallways and footprints on the floor to be decided by students and families, (2) classroom or small group experiences such as bulletin boards, classroom libraries, even what is displayed on the teacher's desk, (3) individual-level of expression such as locker decorating or backpack iron patches. We invite educators to design what your school looks like with the input of students and families. This multiyear project may involve permission from the district and family support. The visuals should also be ever-evolving and open to change after several years. The way a school appears should be reflective of the students inside and the outside world. This can be a community-connecting project and a way to visually demonstrate the schools' mission and vision upon entering the building. If your school is led by an administrator who sees no value in a visually affirming space, you may need to advocate for that administrator to make decisions beyond their personal preferences, especially if students are eager to see this change.

Curricular Progress

Updating your school's curricular offerings may include multiple acts of educational advocacy, depending on your district or institution. The fight is worth it. While some schools have long adopted ethnic studies into their teachings, other schools are not quite able or ready to be more culturally responsive in their areas of content instruction. Progress is still possible. Audit your courses at intervals. This could be every three years or sooner. As the world changes rapidly with the advancement of technology and how students are connected to global happenings and ideas, our teaching and facilitation of knowledge must adjust and adapt.

> In our computer science course, even though we do a lot of individual coding, I created twice as many opportunities for students to engage in groupwork because these next few classes were in upper elementary and middle school when the pandemic hit. They spent a year at home without those group work experiences and so I knew I needed to build that into my teaching more.
>
> (Nineth Grade Computer Science Teacher)

There may be solutions and ideas just up the road at the other local public school or in the mind of a grandparent who remembers a special teacher from their childhood. The goal here is not to outline the ten ways educators can update their lesson plans but to provide all types of educators, counselors, and administrators with the building blocks for re-evaluating what is taught. This will be relevant no matter where you work or what happens in our global society. How the curriculum is evaluated in relationship to what the community needs and what the world needs is key.

Liberation Narratives

We've been here before. History will repeat itself, and we must respond in kind.

During a presentation given by Dr. Kristina Kyles-Smith of the Girls Charter School, Inc. in Maryland, it was stated that liberation narratives are hidden (2024). Liberation narratives are the stories gone missing from our everyday lives. These stories teach us how to separate ourselves from the constraints of society, such as being overworked, feelings of hopelessness, propensity to control students, difficulties with supervisors, and more. Dr. Kyles-Smith urges educators to make these often untold stories visible within their school processes. For example, the life of Fanny Lou Hamer is one of unbridled determination. What lessons can be learned from her life and her life's work around voting rights? As a Black woman with a disability, her story might inspire a special education class on how to self-advocate. She may be a person of study for a middle school social studies class to compare past events with current events. The idea is to find examples of perseverance, especially of marginalized people, and learn directly from their lived experiences. Doing what is not typically done in your school community will further release your school from the binds of the status quo. Building these practices regularly in the learning experience will move you toward progress. Include the history of your community and your own family that can be learned from and strengthened for the future. Amplify the good that has been done and the areas that still need to grow. Make this a staple in your school communications with students and families. What does the program of study say about your institution and its priorities or connection to the community it serves? Make those connections with your students and colleagues and for your families.

We Are Not Saviors

Saviorism is the idea that those in positions of authority have a special role in saving or rescuing others, in this instance, students. These ideas can unknowingly seep into our belief system and our subconscious, causing us to act in ways that dehumanize or delegitimize the strengths and skills our students use every day. Commonly accepted terms to uplift students may actually dehumanize them, such as grit and growth mindset. These terms, while well-intentioned, place the onus of overcoming racism, classism, sexism, homophobia, and other societal ills on students. The idea that students must show us in schools that they are "gritty" or determined despite oppression minimizes the role oppression has in their lives because the students become the focus of how to overcome. Though they do, students shouldn't have to overcome oppression. Adults should eliminate oppression. Students shouldn't have to smile and learn despite being hungry. Adults should provide students with food. Students shouldn't have to be respectful toward an environment that disrespects them. Adults should create better environments. Educators must be aware of student-focused problematizing and compare it to institutions and conditions that create the problems children face. This means the school's problems are the institution's to fix, not the students. While we may encourage students to participate in creating solutions for their schools, educators must recognize that the adults and the institution maintain the status quo, and the status quo doesn't work for all children. Educators are not in schools to save children, and children are not in schools to save educators. The healthiest version of a school can exist where collaboration and innovation are invited, supported, and encouraged, given everyone's unique talents and contributions.

Sustainability

We don't have to choose one or the other. We can have Vygotsky and Ladson-Billings or Bandura and Freire. When we are in constant study and reflection with the brilliant minds of education past and present, we can sustain the practices that help our school communities thrive. The authors of this text are fierce public school advocates and overwhelmingly support the right for every child to be educated in a way that meets their needs and desires. There is also much to be learned from various types of educational spaces. The public vs charter vs private schools debate makes for contention in our nation, but we can learn much from each. Funding aside, which we learned about in previous chapters, the education and support provided must evolve and grow and must assume better practices before all institutions fail our children. What can be learned from private school education? What do they get right? What works for their students? What works for homeschooled children? Where are the inequities, and how are students supported effectively? What isn't possible in public schools that is possible in charter schools? How can we learn from that? Educators should fiercely defend education as a public right, even though public education is a relatively recent national law. Advocacy at all levels will ensure schools have the tools they need to build upon the progress of the past and learn from past mistakes.

Sustainability is how Dr. Kyles-Smith (2024) helps define an empowered community. What's the point of creating a healthy learning environment that lasts only a few school years or changes when the principal leaves? Are we working for the institution or working for the students? Use the technology to help sustain and create plans to maintain progress. Dr. Kyles-Smith invites us to use our technology resources and ask ChatGPT to "Draft a plan to sustain this program for 5 school years" or "Draft a plan for our new principal to continue this program or initiative for the next two school years" and edit based on any adjustments that need to be made.

In the meantime, ask your school community if your institution provides an education for assimilation or education for empowerment. Dr. Kyles-Smith asks educators to rate themselves as educators. Rate your institution. Collecting data is one way to gauge progress but also, identify what seems sustainable given the community's capacity for change. Author and educator, Gholdy Muhammad (2020) writes in her book *Cultivating Genius: An Equity Framework for Culturally and Historically Responsive Literacy* that pursuing urgent understanding is helpful for educators as they begin to better wrestle with and explain inequities in education, stepping toward anti-oppressive practices. She emphasizes humanizing instruction that is compassionate and intellectual. Criticality enables us to question the world and its texts for the truth in history, power, and equity. Her book is an example of what teachers in every school should be looking toward when considering how they will sustain better practices with students. Guides such as this embed sustainability in their creation and implementation. They refocus educators on our purpose and provide practical frameworks for organizing the systems we hope to shift and change.

Ongoing Evaluation and Feedback

Administrators and educators should have a hand in ongoing evaluation and feedback. Studies show that holistic educator evaluations provide more helpful insights to continue on the path of organizational progress. Wake Forest University (n.d.) in North Carolina outlines how schools might embed holistic approaches to educator evaluation. Rubrics and templates are provided to access the comprehensive and human-centered work already vetted by our colleagues throughout the field of education. When federal or state mandates seem to oppose our efforts toward equity and holistic education, educational leaders must find the routes to maintain progress. This requires a commitment to empower educators through the most difficult of times. Scapegoating teachers, counselors, and direct service workers is often an unintentional harm that avoids accountability. With community-minded leaders, the ways educators are evaluated can be influenced by what society suggests but should mostly reflect the established values of the school community. Leaders must remain diligently self-aware and limit instances of blaming and shaming, even when education laws promote ineffective methods of high accountability.

Review these questions with the leaders in your building:

- What definition of professionalism will continue to evolve in your context?

- How will you continue to evaluate, and who will be involved?

- How will you know the educators in your building are empowered to educate children?

- How does leadership promote thriving among educators?

- How will your school community promote family-community engagement in EVERY pursuit, so much so, that it becomes the air you breathe?

- Are teaching strategies and counselor programming aligned with the institutional mission and vision? If so, how? If not, why not? This is your measure.

- Show your work! Invite families, elected officials, and community members into the evaluation process to determine what matters to interest-holders.

Finally, educators and school leaders must create space for community care, mutual aid, and deeper conversations that inspire. Please do not forget taking time away from work!! The gift of time cannot be overstated. Society and the status quo set a standard of production, where workers are depleted in their career environments so that they may not know rest in a nourishing way. Not only do educators need mental, physical, emotional, and spiritual rest, but they need educational leaders who support those resting needs. Each news cycle contains messages about districts that do not trust their employees to respect the boundaries of time. Educational leaders must side with educators and allow time away from the classroom, time away from school, time to heal, time to connect with family, and time to reflect. Educational leaders are responsible for creating the spaces and places needed. Burnout does not have to be inevitable. Take the steps to ensure a healthy working environment.

We hope this text has been helpful. We do not propose we have all the answers to all that plague education. As practicing educators and educational leaders, we felt it imperative to offer our learnings from the past decades. We are adding many practical and doable tools to a plethora of educational knowledge. Our resources are meant to increase your knowledge and improve your practice. Together, we can continue to shape the kind of educational system our children and the world need.

> It means actively working for change, sometimes in the absence of any surety that change is coming. It means doing the unromantic and tedious work necessary to forge meaningful coalitions, and it means recognizing which coalitions are possible

and which coalitions are not. It means knowing that coalition, like unity, means the coming together of whole, self-actualized human beings, focused and believing, not fragmented automatons marching to a prescribed step. It means fighting despair.

(Lorde, 1984, p. 144)

Doing the Work

In each Doing the Work section, we will take the learning from the chapter and apply it to self-work, collaborative work, and professional learning work. To impact change, we must do the work.

Self-Work

Self-reflection questions related to progress should be explored through journaling. Note your personal and professional definitions of progress and consider what led to these ideas. Draw lines connecting to your students' goals and make a separate column for ways in which your ideas of progress may differ from others.

Otherwise Possibilities

What may be another possibility? Have you ever spent 5 minutes drawing a diagram or listing words that remind you of joyful learning and unconditional belonging? Do you even know what that experience is like to conjure an image of it? These questions are designed to help you envision "anew." The concept of otherwise comes from several social and educational researchers in America and abroad where we take the parts of us that may have always felt like we don't belong or hear from people who feel like they don't belong and invite us to sit together and think of something else; something else to be, to dream, to wonder, to fight for, to hold, to use as healing (Awan et al., 2017). Can you imagine educating and counseling an entire school of children who feel and are completely in belonging? Or do you believe that some group of children always have to be marginalized or suffering? Your answer will impact how you proceed with dismantling. Use the reference about otherwise to draft a map of something else.

Collaborative Work

Advocacy in educator prep programs: Connect with an educator preparation program in your region. Collaborate with professors and students to examine the ways in which the system maintains inequities. Continue to collaborate around progress goals for shared accountability. Advocacy groups can be within content areas or areas of practice (i.e., school counselors connect with counselor educators, science teachers connect with biology, chemistry, and physics professors or education professors).

In interest-similar small groups, coordinate efforts with a nonprofit community-based organization in your local area. Plan how you can support each other over 2–3 school years. Define shared goals and remember to keep the students at the forefront of planning.

Professional Learning Work

As a school, identify the barriers that stand in the way of progress. Each professional should further these examples by listing how they contribute to the barriers and help remove them.

As a school, audit the evaluation systems for improvement.

References

Ahmed, S. K. (2018). *Being the change: Lessons and strategies to teach social comprehension.* Heinemann.

Awan, N., Awan, N., & Schalk, M. (2017). Mapping otherwise: Imagining other possibilities and other futures. In *Feminist futures of spatial practice: Materialism, activism, dialogues, pedagogies, projections* (pp. 33–42). AADR/Spurbuchverlag.

Kyles-Smith, K. (2024, August). *Presentation on liberation narratives at the Annual State of Black Education Conference* [Conference presentation].

Lorde, A. (1984). *Sister outsider: Essays & speeches by Audre Lorde.* Crossing Press. 134–144

Minor, C. (2019). *We got this.* Heinemann.

Muhammad, G. E. (2020). *Cultivating Genius: An Equity Framework for Culturally and Historically Responsive Literacy.* Scholastic.

Phung, M. (2015). Asian-Indigenous relationalities: Literary gestures of respect and gratitude. *Canadian Literature,* (227), 56–72.

Ray, V. (2019). A theory of racialized organizations. *American Sociological Review, 84*(1), 26–53.

Wake Forest University. (n.d.). Resources. https://college.wfu.edu/faculty-resources/teachingassessment/resources/#20230423213500

Wood, A. M., Froh, J. J., & Geraghty, A. W. (2010). Gratitude and well-being: A review and theoretical integration. *Clinical Psychology Review, 30*(7), 890–905.

AFTERWORD
RESIST

We submitted our manuscript in early January 2025. Feeling accomplished, we were ready to move to our other interests. And then the United States shifted. Hard. Every day we wake up and are unsure of what is going to happen that day. I (Rebecca) have committed to calling my senators and congresswoman daily, volunteering within my community to mitigate the impact of loss of federal funding and the chaos that is impacting nonprofits, and building a community of people who care and take action.

Last week, my sister texted me in a panic to say that there were Immigration Enforcement (ICE) raids happening all over her city. Her school is predominantly Latino and she was worried about her elementary-aged students going home to find out their parents were gone. Would ICE come to her school? If they did, how could they protect their students?

This week, congresspeople were barred from entering the Department of Education and other federal buildings. We are wondering not only if the Individuals with Disabilities Education Act will be funded but whether we can expect any education-related laws to stay the same.

We have talked through this book about how to stand up for what is right. Typically, we have referenced federal law that will protect students as a way to do so. In light of current events, we don't know if that will hold true. We wanted to add a chapter to the book to help think through how to stand up for students without losing your job. We can't afford to lose educators who care about kids. We can't afford to lose you.

There is a quote that is attributed to Ruth Bader Ginsburg among others but apparently is not attributable to anyone I can find: "When injustice becomes law, resistance becomes duty." The time is now, as educators we have a duty to resist those that would take away the rights of our students and their families.

Resist: What Does That Mean?

When I am overwhelmed by the world, I often feel that there's nothing that I can do to stand up to the tidal wave of negativity. I'm not brave enough or smart enough or informed enough to really do something. In an earlier chapter, we explored educators in history who stood up for what's right as changemakers. It is so helpful to look for the good in our history and study how to replicate it. History always repeats itself, right?

Let's use an example that is known by all: Rosa Parks. Rosa Parks refused to move from her seat on the bus, igniting the Birmingham Bus Boycotts, a pivotal moment in the civil rights movement. When I was younger, we learned that Ms. Parks was "tired that day." In fact, it was a coordinated movement by the Women's Political Council that started years before the boycott (The Martin Luther King, Jr. Research and Education Institute, n.d.).

Maybe you think, I could never do something like that, I'm not brave enough! Think about all of the people who were involved in the boycott: people who copied and distributed flyers or who gave rides to those without cars and the employers who didn't fire their employees for being late. I've heard stories of people who cooked meals for those whose work days were suddenly much longer without a bus. It was a community effort.

As educators, we can be a part of a community effort to protect our students. What are the talents and skills that you have and can contribute? A friend of mine mentioned that she can't risk being arrested at a protest because she is the sole provider for her child. Another friend mentioned that she can't donate money to certain organizations because of her wife's security clearance. They both went on to talk about what they've done instead.

Alicia and I have a saying: little by little but don't stop. The time is now.

Another often misattributed quote is apt for this very moment: "If not you, who? If not now, when?" – Hillel the Elder. I (Alicia) am transparent about my political affiliations and leanings. My priorities since my first vote at the age of 18 were to protect democracy, protect marginalized communities, and support students as they pursue their goals. During the past few months, which often feel like years, I have seen many Black women like me stand for justice only to be met with unsurprising yet still disappointing decisions from our neighbors, friends, and colleagues. We have to move forward with those who have the same vision: a just society.

There have always been people who have fought for justice for those most crushed by systems in America. Those are the people I recall when I consider turning away from critical action. The unity of people, of all races, is what will carry us through our most difficult moments. We all need to assess our strengths and act for the betterment of our future. There is no justice without all of us contributing as much as we can.

How to Start

The best thing you can do is keep up to date on what is happening at the federal, state, and local levels with education specifically. It can be hard to keep up with the news when you are inundated with negativity. We recommend that you find a few reputable sources and protect your sanity by checking them on a schedule. I like to check in at the end of the work day but not in the morning when it really brings down my mood for the whole day.

Pay attention to anything that dismantles individual rights as well. While not an education policy or law per se, trans rights, women's rights, immigrant rights are all topics that impact our students deeply.

Find Your Community

You cannot do this alone. Finding a community gives you a space for comfort and support in times when many are, understandably, feeling scared for their future, the future of their students, and the country in general. If you don't have a community of educators within your own building, find a way to build it. Alicia and I met on Twitter years ago and I am better for my connection to her. If you have a local educator's association or union, you might find a community there. Maybe your community is individuals from outside the educators within your area but are deeply invested.

Be careful that your community includes folks who are deeply knowledgeable about education. I have many people in my personal community who rely on me as their educator expert. This is great! I'm happy to help. But it doesn't give me a sense of having others who are in this with me.

We also need a community because it allows us to see the amplification of our work. When I am feeling helpless, it helps me to see that others are also making an effort. If we add all of our efforts together, it increases exponentially. My connection with others builds my ability to keep going both through a sense of community and through visibly seeing my efforts amplified by the work of the whole.

Know Your Why

Have you seen the joke about needing some "precedented times." I discovered there's even a whole Etsy page dedicated to items with jokes about precedented times printed on them. Y'all, this is exhausting. If I really wanted to, I could probably pull the covers up over my head and ignore what's happening in our country.

When I was in college, I worked tutoring a student with autism. His mom was a single mom who was also a cardiothoracic surgeon. She had two children, one of whom needed a significant level of support. She would always say that she didn't read the news because she didn't have time to worry about that. I get it, I really do. I wonder if she feels differently now that students with disabilities may lose their rights. I imagine she does.

When you have a why, you know where to focus your efforts. You can protect yourself by finding a laser-like focus on your issues. If the house is on fire, you can't personally save it all. For me, that issue is education and students. I remain informed and caring on many issues but my actions are mostly confined to issues related to students.

Consider these questions:

- What are your personal strengths? Consider how they can be helpful to those who are most negatively impacted.

- Include your loved ones. What areas might your close neighbor, cousin, or nephew focus their efforts? What skills can they bring to creating more fair and transparent systems? How can you begin talking to them about it?

- What keeps you from acting? Take inventory of your personal barriers and work with a thought partner on solutions to each barrier.

- Pause for self-assessment. How does it physically feel when you are ready for action? What does fear of action feel like? How does it feel mentally and emotionally? What might provide meaningful relief so that you can act despite your fears?

- What privileges allow you to turn away from action? How can you channel those privileges for someone else's benefit?

Make a Plan

As a district leader in student services, I am a part of the response team that is deployed to schools that have had a tragedy. One of my former colleagues in a larger district, who responded to hundreds of tragedies per school year, always commented that she could tell when a school had done some planning before tragedy struck. When we have high emotions, when we feel unsafe, when we are pulled in many directions, we aren't as great at responding.

Here are some questions to get you started:

- What is your issue that you want to address?

- Who are the decision-makers in that area? Think about the quadrants of influence we explored earlier in the book.

- What is your bandwidth for action? Can you make some phone calls, attend a board meeting, fly to Washington to meet with your senator? Every effort matters and is important.

- What action are you committed to taking?

- What preparation is needed to take that action?

- How will you know when you have successfully completed the action? What is the outcome you are seeking?

Advocacy

Just about everything I have read about the actions of early 2025 is that the purpose is to stifle response from the public because they are overwhelmed with what is happening. I believe that hopelessness is the goal. Even before this new effort to dismantle the government, we have seen a shift in the way that the general public, decision-makers, and leaders feel about education.

Don't we want to help children? Isn't a well-informed public the goal? Aren't we better off if we have a democracy full of critical thinkers? Well, maybe. While some would argue that the answer to these questions is no, I think generally, people do care about kids and want them to have an education. So why aren't they helping educators? In recent times, we have seen the vilification of educators. Even Meghan Trainor famously said "F- teachers" on her podcast (NBC News, 2023).

I've been thinking a lot recently about why education feels so much worse than it used to. As a veteran educator, I can fullheartedly say that working in the profession has gotten worse over my 22 years. I think it's because the general public no longer respects educators as having specialized knowledge and skills for educating children. This happens not just outside the walls of the school but within them as well. Research says that is exactly what is happening with a steady decline beginning in 2010 (Kraft & Lyon, 2024).

All of this leads to more and more despair over the future of education. The opposite of despair? Action. Imagine yourself in despair. What are you doing? I think of myself lying in bed, covers wrapped around me, feeling like doing anything is pointless. Trust me, this has literally happened in the last few months. Now, imagine yourself in action. What are you doing? I think of myself moving purposefully, looking smart and ready to do something. I am poised to spring into a response at any moment. It *feels* different than despair. It feels like action.

Make Connections

By definition, advocacy happens through interacting with those who have the power to influence decisions. As an educator, you are used to advocacy! You have been doing this for your whole career. When I want to start a program at my school, I advocate for how it's going to impact the School Improvement Plan. When I wanted to do a schoolwide day celebrating kids, I advocated with teachers about why it was worth the work.

Recently, I was accepted to be a fellow in the Education Policy Fellowship through the North Carolina Public School Forum. This program teaches educators, education supporters, and nonprofit organization leaders about how education policy is made at the state and local levels. As part of this experience, we spent a week in Washington, learning from Washington insiders who are education advocates and visiting our lawmakers to advocate ourselves.

This was a truly transformative experience for me. Not only did it fill my soul in a time of desperation wondering what was happening in our country at the beginning of 2025, but it was amazing to be surrounded by other people who were as deeply passionate about educators and students. If you ever have the opportunity to participate in something like this, seize it. There are education policy fellowships happening all around the United States.

One profound but simple takeaway that I had from my time in Washington was to be nice and human. Sometimes when we speak with people in power, we might be nervous or overly formal. We might feel compelled to have a speech prepared. In reality, people in power are often used to people being angry with them. When you come in on the offensive, they become defensive.

Even when meeting with people who are very different from you in their opinions and actions, it's important to make a connection. When in Washington, we met with staffers of lawmakers we had never voted for. Lawmakers whose voting record differed from my beliefs vastly. However, in order to sway their vote, we need to make a connection. One way to do that is to build rapport. Share a little about yourself, and find ways that you relate to the person you are speaking to.

Be Useful

Advocacy is a long game. One of the ways that you build trust with decision-makers is to be useful to them. As a central office leader for school counselors, I encourage my counselors to take the work they do in the school counseling program and "translate" it to what their principal cares about. They want to start a new peer mentoring program? How will it improve attendance, behavior, or academic performance?

Leaders and decision-makers, just like lawmakers, are responsible for a large number of things. They can't always stay informed on all the topics they are in charge of leading. Your job as an advocate for your work is to make sure you keep them informed about the important information. As an employee myself, I always strive for my supervisors to feel like if I'm in charge of it, they don't need to worry about it – I've got it handled! Then when I do come to them, I haven't used up the bandwidth they can give me for simple things and can advocate for the big ideas.

Think about a decision-maker that you would like to advocate with. Maybe it's a school board member who always votes against programs that would support the students at your school. Maybe it's your principal that doesn't prioritize something you think is vital to your work. Maybe it's even a parent that you'd like to engage more in their child's education. How can you make their life easier? How can you be useful to them?

To do that, we need to consider what interests, motivates, and concerns the person you are advocating with.

Decentering Yourself

Making space for the advocacy of others requires a focus on students and other decision-makers. Ask yourself the following questions and take steps toward an action-oriented approach:

1. In what ways do I collaborate best with other decision-makers?
2. Are there relationships decision-makers have with others that I can learn from?
3. What might stand in the way of you forging or bridging an advocacy-related relationship with other decision-makers?
4. Are you practiced at "getting out of your own way"? This means that you recognize the barriers and limitations you have when collaborating with others. We all have them. Do you know yours?
5. Where can you get support to address your personal and professional barriers and limitations? Who can help you attend to your needs for the sake of the advocacy efforts?

An example of this occurred when I, Alicia Oglesby, submitted a proposal to hire a school counseling intern to assist in the school and college counseling office. The proposal was postponed and I was personally annoyed and professionally deflated. I saw the impact of having an intern at previous schools and knew my current school could benefit greatly from having someone in that role. Generally, I collaborate best with decision-makers when our ideas are shared but this wasn't the case. I saw how decision-makers interacted with various educators and knew that I needed to "get out of my own way" by playing the long game, being persistent, but also being gentle in my approach. Ultimately, an intern would strengthen our office's ability to advocate for students particularly because the intern candidate had a background in working with marginalized youth. The effort is worth the strategy and the battle. By centering the students, I was able to depersonalize the postponement and keep my focus on the issue: hiring an intern.

This is a minor concern in the grand scheme of all issues students face, especially at a time in our society where students are being kept from culturally relevant literature, accosted on the sports field for their gender identity, and in danger of losing life-altering accommodations. Advocacy around these issues makes you useful to the decision-makers who have to fight for accommodations, fair athletics experiences, and access to books. Show that you can do both: fight for what is right and be a team player.

Difference Is Our Defense

Educators don't have to be the same to collaborate and promote positive outcomes for students. Each day, teachers, counselors, administrators, and staff model how to coexist even when our backgrounds, family dynamics, communication styles, and professional identities are different. Differences can not hinder action. Each day is an opportunity to work at better understanding each other so that we can act on behalf and alongside students. Educators should also be aware of the ways in which students teach us to be better adults. As long as we are learning from each other, we can stay current on the needs of children and the needs of our schools.

Consider:

1. How you are different from other decision-makers in your school community?
2. What these differences mean for your ability to collaborate?
3. Addressing these differences head-on. Don't let the elephant in the room stay there. As you prepare to precondition for action, practice bringing any awkwardness or distance to the forefront. Practice the language you might use. For example, "Hey Nicole, I know we haven't really spoken much since I started working here and we don't really have a strong work relationship, but I'd like to work with you on something and I hope you will be open to the possibility."
4. Leaning into your differences to enter into a collaboration by showing decision-makers how certain differences complement or supplement each other.

Precondition to Action

How many times have you gone to a person, shared your thoughts, and they said, "You know what? You're right, I think I'm going to completely change what I'm doing and follow that." Probably never. Maybe once or twice. That's not how people make decisions!

When we're advocating for big changes, we have to think about the space from knowledge to action as a continuum. At the beginning, the person may be completely unaware of what you're talking about. Let's think of the example of the school board member who votes against a program that you care deeply about. Let's say it's to budget for transportation for after-school tutoring. The board member thinks it's a waste of money because not that many students will use the provided transportation.

In that instance, you would want to share with them the unintended consequences of cutting this transportation. That our most vulnerable students would be unable to participate in the tutoring program. That even though the majority of our students in our district use the school bus, of the students who participate in tutoring, the vast majority do.

We have advocated to move that school board member from being completely unaware to aware. But they might not really understand the implications. That if we cut transportation, we de facto cut the entire program. Students who need it most, won't be able to participate. This isn't an inconvenience to families but a cut of a critical service.

Now the school board member gets it but they're still not sure that the added expense is worth it when the district is struggling with finances. They are asking for more information on the right approach. Their hands are tied, they can't do anything about it. The budget is what the budget is. They have moved from comprehended to convinced. Conviction does not equal action.

The final step is to relate the action you need to the person who will make the action. You know that the school board member is one who ran on the platform that they want to improve reading scores. If the district changes the tutoring program from being for kids who need it to kids who can provide their own transportation, the changes we want to see in reading scores might not happen.

This last step is the most crucial. When you need an action from another person, you have to connect the conviction to them and their interests, motivations, and concerns. There's a big difference between I won't stand in your way and I will actively help you.

Think about that decision-maker you considered earlier. Where do they stand on your issue? How can you move them to one spot?

- Unaware
- Aware
- Comprehends
- Convinced
- Action

Once you have your decision-maker committed to an action, it's time to give them a decision ready-made for them. They are busy, they might not have time to consider what they actually need to do. Tread carefully here, as we discussed in an earlier chapter, some leaders will balk at being told what to do and will be contrary to any decision you share.

Many leaders will make decisions based on effectiveness. How likely am I to see the change I am seeking through the strategy this person is bringing me. They are looking for the most effective way to get to their goal. In this effectiveness algorithm, they are also considering logistics and amount of effort in their calculations. If the program is likely to be very effective, they might not mind a higher level of effort and logistics. Where can they get the best bang for their buck?

Other leaders will be thinking about relevance. How relevant to my top issues is this proposal? Great leaders can't afford to be distracted by every fun and exciting project. The only way to reach the goal is to stay focused. This is a tricky one because the topic is usually very relevant to you. It can be frustrating when something you see as so important is not considered relevant to the decision-maker. That's when you start thinking about how you can "translate" your concern into a topic of relevance for them.

Lastly, other leaders might be thinking about the popularity of the action you are requesting. When I started in one of my roles, there was very little institutional trust in the position I was taking. I could be the very best candidate and do my very best job but people were already unlikely to trust what I did because of how they felt about my predecessors. I had to think very carefully about how popular my decisions were in this beginning stage. Once I had built trust with my staff, I was able to move away from popularity. Popularity isn't always a bad thing and can often be a truly legitimate concern.

In reality, most leaders are thinking of some combination of the three when considering whether to act. We might never know their true decision-making model but it is helpful to consider these three topics when you are working to move a decision-maker into action.

Consider these questions for effectiveness, relevant, and popularity:

Effectiveness
1. What data can you show that will illuminate your effort or plan?
2. Do you have a history to draw from of effective practices? Use this as your credibility.

Relevance
1. How can you demonstrate how this plan will be impactful for your students?
2. Do you have student and family input? Do you have their permission to quote them?

3. Can you concisely connect the dots for decision-makers through visualizations, easy-to-understand graphs, or testimonials?
4. How is this plan relevant to the decision-maker?

Popularity

1. Do you have buy-in from others in the community? If so, how can this be captured and demonstrated?
2. How might the popularity of the plan benefit the decision-maker or relieve pressure on another initiative that they prioritize?

Advocacy: A Final Word

Good advocacy takes careful planning. I am often a wing-it kind of person who feels comfortable walking into many situations without preparation. However, to truly advocate well, you do need to have a plan. But you also don't want to have too much of a plan. It's a real Goldilocks situation. Be natural, know your decision-maker, and think through your talking points before you arrive.

3*2*1 Talking Points:

- What are 3 main ideas you want to make sure to get across?
- What 2 questions would you like to ask of the decision-maker?
- What is you 1 ask as you close the meeting?

Resistance

Sometimes despite our best attempts at advocacy, changes are made that you ethically disagree with. We've talked a bit about some of these times in the book so far. At the time of this writing, we don't really know what is going to happen at a federal level in the United States, but we are aware that we may be asked to do things counter to our beliefs. This might include outing a transgender student, requesting immigration status upon enrollment, or removing DEI initiatives from the work that we do.

In that situation, we need to be able to resist with more than persuasion. We have some ideas that we think might help. Make sure that you check your own school district's rules and regulations as well as the law. "Learn the rules so you know how to break them politically, ethically and legally" (American School Counselor Association (ASCA), n.d.).

Don't Rush

I would say that many educators are fairly compliant. We work within a system that highly values compliance, perhaps sometimes to a fault. When we get a request from an authority figure, we typically try to respond quickly. For example, if your school were to receive a subpoena from a lawyer, they would likely reply in a timely manner.

As we move into a time of uncertainty, we need to remember to slow down and ensure that we are doing what's right not just what's been requested. Let's say that an ICE officer came to your school and asked for records. What do you do next? I have a saying: we'll follow the law but you need to too. If ICE were to come to the building (at the time of this writing that has not happened yet), make sure you slow down and check all of the steps in order to only do what you are legally required to do. FERPA applies to all students and they deserve to have their legal protections maintained.

Sometimes we can also use the "don't rush" to slow down the process when we've been asked to do something we disagree with. In January 2025, the Oklahoma State Board of Education proposed that schools should collect data related to immigration status when students enroll in school (Associated Press, 2025). At schools where I've worked, we've seen things in the headlines and assumed they are going to happen. We might want to get a head start on the ask that will be coming our way.

In this case, if you were to rush and implement this idea before it became a policy or procedure, you would be causing potential harm to students when not actually required to do so. At the time of this writing, the governor of Oklahoma has rejected this plan which will likely stall it moving forward (Levenson, 2025). I wonder how many schools are collecting this data or keeping notes "just in case." Be cautious about being too overeager to comply.

We can also hurt students and families by working quickly to comply with directives that we find morally or ethically inappropriate. Parents Bill of Rights laws may direct you to out transgender students to their parents. Before implementing this expectation, find out what the legal parameters really are by consulting your district staff or asking for written guidance that has been vetted by a lawyer. Slowing down this implementation will give kids time to adapt and will make sure that when you do have to act, you are doing only what is required of you.

Finally, implement these procedures to the letter. Don't provide short-cuts that make it easier to implement. In our state, we have a Parents Bill of Rights law that requires parents to be notified of any alternative name a student may go by. Because of this, I give the guidance that we include any and all students who don't go by exactly what their legal name is. A William who goes by Will has their parents sign the form. If we only implement names that we think are unusual or that indicate a different gender, we are othering students who don't fit into the norm that we expect.

Recently the unclassified CIA document *Simple Sabotage Field Manual*, used during World War II to teach subversion to Nazi detractors has been making the rounds. To quote their advice "Be as irritable and quarrelsome as possible without getting yourself in trouble" (Office of Strategic Services, 1944, p. 31)

So how will you stand up and resist when you see wrong doing being done to education system, to our teachers, to our students? May you be as irritable and quarrelsome as possible. But don't get into too much trouble, we need you here in education.

Take care of yourself and your students,

Rebecca & Alicia

References

American School Counselor Association (ASCA). (n.d.). *Appropriate vs. inappropriate duties*. Retrieved February 25, 2025, from https://www.schoolcounselor.org/Magazines/September-October-2017/Appropriate-vs-Inappropriate-Duties

Associated Press. (2025, January 29). Oklahoma schools plan to require proof of students' immigration status. *The Guardian*. https://www.theguardian.com/us-news/2025/jan/28/oklahoma-schools-immigration-status

Kraft, M. A., & Lyon, M. A. (2024). *The rise and fall of the teaching profession: Prestige, interest, preparation, and satisfaction over the last half century* (Working Paper No. 32386). National Bureau of Economic Research. https://doi.org/10.3386/w32386

Levenson, E. (2025, February 24). *Oklahoma governor rejects plan to ask students about immigration status and slams 'political drama' at Board of Education*. CNN. https://www.cnn.com/2025/02/24/us/oklahoma-education-immigration/index.html

NBC News. (2023, April 24). Meghan Trainor apologized for dissing teachers. Some say they're still upset. https://www.nbcnews.com/pop-culture/meghan-trainor-teacher-apology-backlash-rcna81209

Office of Strategic Services. (1944). *Simple sabotage field manual* (No. No. 3; pp. 1–32).

The Martin Luther King, Jr. Research and Education Institute. (n.d.). Montgomery *bus boycott*. Retrieved February 8, 2025, from https://kinginstitute.stanford.edu/montgomery-bus-boycott

INDEX

Note: page references in *italics* denote figures.

For Product Safety Concerns and Information please contact our EU
representative GPSR@taylorandfrancis.com
Taylor & Francis Verlag GmbH, Kaufingerstraße 24, 80331 München, Germany

www.ingramcontent.com/pod-product-compliance
Lightning Source LLC
Chambersburg PA
CBHW050656280326
41932CB00015B/2926

9 7 8 1 0 3 2 7 1 7 4 1 8